My Anchor Holds ove

I Took It Personally

By Josmamie Thomas

Contents

Introduction

Allow me to hearten you. If you are reading this book, you probably have a broken heart and are bewildered about your current family circumstances, especially if you tried to parent correctly. Do not be dismayed; God has a remedy for all situations, and He is faithful.

This book is a tribute to the power and faithfulness of Jesus Christ to raise up a ministry, the Anchor Academy for Boys, for the purpose of saving our future . . . God's mighty men of valor (our sons). God uses the Anchor to thwart the enemy of our souls in his tracks by ardently instituting biblical character-building principles in the lives of wavering young men.

I would like to share with you several points and excerpts from my logbooks, and reference Scriptures we prayed through as God was in the process of delivering our son from the grips of Satan. It is our prayer that all of you will be comforted and encouraged as you stand back and witness the salvation of the Lord.

Philippians 1:6 says, "Being confident of this very thing, that he which hath begun a good work in you will perform it until the day of Jesus Christ."

Do not lose heart. God is not yet finished with your son!

Chapter 1

Hope for a Future

Point One: Getting Off the Throne!

"Rebellion" is a dirty word in our Western culture and is shunned almost as much as the word "sin." Critics of moral/Judeo-Christian values would argue that like the smallpox disease, both are nonexistent and have been eradicated. I would beg to differ. Smallpox is a serious, contagious, and sometimes fatal infectious disease. Likewise, rebellion against God and those in authority is serious, contagious, and sometimes fatal. There is currently no cure for smallpox—although the vaccine can sometimes help those recently exposed. Unlike smallpox, there is a treatment for sin and rebellion. That treatment would be salvation by God through the Lord Jesus Christ.

When your sons, daughters, or even you are on the throne of the heart, then the Lord Jesus is not. Sin is estrangement from God; rebellion is active opposition to God and those in authoritative positions over us. The world teaches that we do not have to revere either, and unfortunately, so many believe the lie, not realizing that God will not share His glory with anyone. An unknown author put it this way: "Sin will take you further than you want to go, keep you longer than you want to stay and cost you more than you want to pay."

Jesus is the ultimate Redeemer, and Satan is the ultimate rebeller. Isaiah 14:12-15 maps out what the influence of the spirit of rebellion is like:

> How art thou fallen from heaven, O Lucifer, son of the morning! how art thou cut down to the ground, which didst weaken the nations! For thou hast said in thine heart, I will ascend into heaven, I will exalt my throne above the stars of God: I will sit also upon the mount of the congregation, in the sides of the north: I will ascend above the heights of the clouds; I will be like the most High. Yet thou shalt be brought down to hell, to the sides of the pit.

Rebellion may rule for a season, but it ultimately will be cut down. Rebellion says, "I will ascend. I will exalt my throne. I will, I will, I will . . . . I will be like the Most High!" However, the truth is, rebellion will be brought down to hell, to the sides of the pit, and rebellion attempts to take everyone and everything with it as it goes down. Don't let it happen!

Our challenge as parents is not to take it personally, but instead to remain focused, steadfast in prayer, mirroring what Jesus would do in such a situation and remembering that whenever we or our children sin, we sin against almighty God in the presence of other people.

Our focus becomes blurred because we have visceral ties to our children, and if we attempted to parent correctly, we allow the enemy to torment us with the ever lamenting, "Oh, God! Where did I go wrong?" Allow me to comfort you; God is the most loving Parent ever, and Adam and Eve rebelled against Him!

When Nathan accosted David about his adultery with Bathsheba and the murder of her husband, Uriah the Hittite,

King David lamented, "I have sinned against the LORD" (2 Samuel 12:13). (It is not that David did not hurt himself and many peripheral people by sinning against God; the truth is quite the contrary.) Just like the sin of Adam and Eve affected all of mankind, David's sin caused the sword never to leave his home: "Now therefore the sword shall never depart from thine house; . . . . Thus saith the LORD" (2 Samuel 12:10-11).

Beloved, our hope and faith is in this: "The sacrifices of God are a broken spirit: a broken and a contrite heart, O God, thou wilt not despise" (Psalm 51:17). To be contrite means to feel or express pain or sorrow for sins or offenses. After being challenged by Nathan (we all need to have a Nathan in our lives), David was contrite in heart. He repented before God, and God forgave him. David got off the throne of his heart. Nevertheless, there were still consequences for his rebellion and disobedience. There is a penalty for sin.

When we rebel against God, we take a privilege that is not ours to take. We were bought for a price: "Ye are bought with a price; be not ye the servants of men" (1 Corinthians 7:23). By rebelling against God, we willfully disobey the only One who is our Source of provision, promise, and protection. The ironic thing is, we take what is not ours to take, and we give it (our rebellion against God) to someone (the devil) who knows exactly what to do with it—"to steal, and to kill, and to destroy" (John 10:10).

All of this would be a sad state of affairs if there were no redeemer. To redeem means to regain possession of by payment of a specific amount. Jesus the Christ is our Redeemer. Once we give ground to the devil, it is only the Lord Jesus who can take it back.

The Anchor Academy will minister effectively to your son the realization that the only hope that we have is when we get off the throne of our hearts and allow Jesus to rule.

Point Two: Dealing With Childishness

Just as our children possess characteristics of childishness, we, as parents, have an obligation to "train up" our children so that the childishness does not turn dangerous down the road.

It is characteristic of children to:

- Be dependent on parents: "But we were gentle among you, even as a nurse cherisheth her children" (1 Thessalonians 2:7).
- Be unstable: "That we henceforth be no more children, tossed to and fro, and carried about with every wind of doctrine, by the sleight of men, and cunning craftiness, whereby they lie in wait to deceive" (Ephesians 4:14).
- Have need for instruction: "Train up a child in the way he should go: and when he is old, he will not depart from it" (Proverbs 22:6).
- Have an influence on adults: "Can a woman forget her sucking child, that she should not have compassion on the son of her womb? yea, they may forget, yet will I not forget thee" (Isaiah 49:15).
- Be foolish: "Foolishness is bound in the heart of a child; but the rod of correction shall drive it far from him" (Proverbs 22:15).
- Be immature: "When I was a child, I spake as a child, I understood as a child, I thought as a child: but when I became a man, I put away childish things" (1 Corinthians 13:11).

It is a parent's obligation to:

- Provide nourishment: "But Hannah went not up; for she said unto her husband, I will not go up until the child be weaned, and then I will bring him, that he

may appear before the LORD, and there abide for ever" (1 Samuel 1:22).
- Provide instruction: "Brethren, I beseech you, be as I am; for I am as ye are: ye have not injured me at all" (Galatians 4:12).
- Help obtain employment: "But David went and returned from Saul to feed his father's sheep at Bethlehem" (1 Samuel 17:15).
- Provide an inheritance: "And one of the company said unto him, Master, speak to my brother, that he divide the inheritance with me. And he said unto him, Man, who made me a judge or a divider over you?" (Luke 12:13-14).
- Provide discipline: "And, ye fathers, provoke not your children to wrath: but bring them up in the nurture and admonition of the Lord" (Ephesians 6:4).

However, childishness is a behavior that can happen at any age, and at any age, it is potentially dangerous ... *It's all about "me, me, me"!*

Childishness was manifested by Saul: "And Saul was very wroth, and the saying displeased him; and he said, They have ascribed unto David ten thousands, and to me they have ascribed but thousands: and what can he have more but the kingdom? And Saul eyed David from that day and forward" (1 Samuel 18:8-9).

King Saul became jealous of David's acclaim with Israel, and it eventually drove King Saul insane. Childishness can happen at any age and is a first cousin to jealousy, envy, strife, and confusion. Scripture tells us, "For where envying and strife is, there is confusion and every evil work" (James 3:16). Our responsibility as parents must be to "check" such behaviors because sin begets sin.

In an article listed on The Gospel Way Web site titled "Is It Unloving to Spank Our Children?" the writer expresses that spanking actually shows love, giving what is needed, and is therefore beneficial. Proverbs 13:24 says: "He who spares his rod hates his son, but he who loves him disciplines him promptly."

At the Anchor, your sons will come through the fire as pure gold.

Point Three: Guarding Against Child-Centricity

Our Western culture is extremely child-centric, and this ought not to be. Yes, children are a blessing from God. "Children's children are the crown of old men; and the glory of children are their fathers" (Proverbs 17:6). However, it is not all about them! Even secular people are realizing that centralizing everything around our children has produced narcissistic, selfish, self-absorbed individuals. These same individuals, bantering situational ethics mantras wherever they go, are integrating into corporations and the political realm. Ergo, we are experiencing the madness of our harvest in the types of ridiculous immoral laws instituted in the United States. God have mercy (not getting what we deserve) on us for committing this sin!

Family hierarchy should be made clear. Married parents, a widowed parent, single parents, grandparents, and guardians with children live under the same hierarchy . . . God comes first! Children have to be taught that there is divine protection, provision, and promise in living out this order.

They are not in charge! You are in charge! Part of the program at the Anchor is retrofitting family roles that have become distorted.

Point Four: Having a Change of Heart

"He was such a loving, pleasant, beautiful baby. What happened to him?" The answer is, "Sin." Be it drugs, sex, or rock 'n' roll, what happened to him was sin, and it singed his mind and heart.

The book of Romans often is referred to as the apostle Paul's greatest work. In it the apostle explores the significance of our Savior's sacrificial death. As saints of God, we love to recite Romans 1:16-17: "For I am not ashamed of the gospel of Christ: for it is the power of God unto salvation to every one that believeth; to the Jew first, and also to the Greek. For therein is the righteousness of God revealed from faith to faith: as it is written, The just shall live by faith."

I would venture to say that we all understand Romans 1:1-17. However, we are sometimes not totally clear about Romans 1:18-32. We understand that there is a reason for and result of guilt of unbelievers, who deny the existence and righteousness of God. However, we unfortunately become confused when we think that God is repeating Himself. Romans 1:24-29 talks about the abominable things mankind approves of and does with mankind. Romans 1:30-31 talks to your situation.

Your son's behavior toward you is unnatural. Natural affection between parents and their children is love, honor, and respect for each other. Your son is acting unnaturally toward you with hate, contempt, and betrayal. Romans 1:30-31 refers to "backbiters, haters of God, despiteful, proud, boasters, inventors of evil things, disobedient to parents, without understanding, covenantbreakers, without natural affection, implacable, unmerciful." Does this resemble your situation?

The teaching, preaching, and demonstration of the love and power of Jesus Christ at the Anchor will compel your son to have a change of heart.

Point Five: "Stand Therefore"

If you are a believer in Jesus Christ, you are equipped through and positioned in Christ to win. If you do not know the Lord Jesus Christ as Savior and Lord, you do not have someone to champion your cause, and you will not be successful in this fight. You do realize you're in a fight, don't you?

If you are not a believer in Christ and would like to become a follower of the Lord Jesus Christ, pray a prayer like this:

"Dear Lord, I realize I am a sinner in need of a Savior. I confess with my mouth and believe in my heart that Jesus Christ, God incarnate, born of a virgin, came to earth, lived a sinless life, and paid my sin debt by dying in my stead on a cross, and God raised Him from the dead. Please forgive me of my sins, come into my heart, and write my name in the Lamb's Book of Life. It is in Jesus' name, I pray. Amen."

If you feel that you're not ready to accept this awesome gift just yet, please read on. We trust as you continue to share our journey, the Holy Spirit will minister to you, and you will turn from your way of thinking and turn to God's way of doing things.

Ephesians 6:1-14(a) sums it up this way:

[1] Children, obey your parents in the Lord: for this is right. [2] Honour thy father and mother; which is the first commandment with promise; [3] That it may be well with thee, and thou mayest live long on the earth. [4] And, ye fathers, provoke not your children to wrath: but bring them up in the nurture and admonition of the Lord. [5] Servants, be obedient to them that are your masters according to the flesh, with fear and trembling, in singleness of your heart, as unto Christ; [6] Not with eyeservice, as menpleasers;

but as the servants of Christ, doing the will of God from the heart; [7]With good will doing service, as to the Lord, and not to men: [8]Knowing that whatsoever good thing any man doeth, the same shall he receive of the Lord, whether he be bond or free. [9]And, ye masters, do the same things unto them, forbearing threatening: knowing that your Master also is in heaven; neither is there respect of persons with him. [10]Finally, my brethren, be strong in the Lord, and in the power of his might. [11]Put on the whole armour of God, that ye may be able to stand against the wiles of the devil. [12]For we wrestle not against flesh and blood, but against principalities, against powers, against the rulers of the darkness of this world, against spiritual wickedness in high places. [13]Wherefore take unto you the whole armour of God, that ye may be able to withstand in the evil day, and having done all, to stand. [14]Stand therefore, . . .

Looking at verses 10-14(a), we see what we, as followers of Christ, need to know for the fight of our children's lives!

First, you must remember that even though your heart is breaking at this present time, you win in the end. The joy of the Lord is your strength, and it is His power and might that makes you strong enough to bear it.

Secondly, the apostle Paul is studying the armor of a Roman soldier who was assigned to guard him in prison. The apostle, writing to the church in Ephesus, tells them that every vital organ must be covered. You must put on the entire Word of God daily in prayer and supplication to the Lord, and the Lord Jesus has your back. "Surely goodness and mercy shall follow you all the days of your life." The armor covers your front. Surely goodness and mercy shall follow you all the days of your lives—that's the Lord Jesus!

Thirdly, remember that you fight the good fight of faith; you "wrestle not against flesh and blood, but against principalities, against powers, against the rulers of the darkness of this world, against spiritual wickedness in high places." Your son is not your enemy; the spiritual influence (i.e., the devil and His minions) is your enemy.

Fourthly, put on the armor so that you can stand. Put on the loin belt of truth; it is the Word of God, your Bible. It is the first part of the ensemble that must be in place for all the other parts of the armor to fit. Put on the breastplate of righteousness (cover your heart so that it won't break). Your feet must be rooted and grounded in the Word of God to the point that you will not be moved no matter what valley you may go through with your boy. The Roman soldier's shoes had six-inch spikes to assure that they would not lose ground for every step they took. Don't be moved! Take the shield of faith with you at all times. The shield can deflect the enemies' fiery darts as they attempt to penetrate your breastplate and burn your heart in anguish. Put on the breastplate of righteousness!

The enemy of your soul wages war against your mind.

> [1] I beseech you therefore, brethren, by the mercies of God, that ye present your bodies a living sacrifice, holy, acceptable unto God, which is your reasonable service. [2] And be not conformed to this world: but be ye transformed by the renewing of your mind, that ye may prove what is that good, and acceptable, and perfect, will of God.
>
> Romans 12:1-2

Use the Word of God as a two-edged sword to cut going in and cut going out. Declare those things that are not as if they were. You've got to believe that nothing is too hard for God!

Finally, when you've done all to stand, stand therefore!

We are praying for your strength in the Lord as you read this book.

I'd like to share this related entry from my journal, written June 22, 2002:

"I just completed a letter to my precious and dear son, Alistair, encouraging him on the stand that he took recently against himself and the enemy of our souls. God is an awesome wonder in how He has redeemed Alistair (in Jesus' name!) from the snare of the fouler. God has done great things! Glory to God forevermore!"

Chapter 2

The Incident

On Friday, August 24, 2001, I wrote in my journal: My God is awesome! As I think about the blood, knife, stitches, and His pending ten-year incarceration, I choose to offer up a sacrifice of praise for the things God has done!

Thursday night was horror personified! Leading up to the act, we were telling Alistair that we were disappointed in him for not pressing his way to go to football practice. On Wednesday evening, we told him that we would not be able to take off work and drive him to practice at 1 P.M. on Thursday, August 23, 2001. Practice would be all day, and then in the evening, the boys and their parents would have a picnic and discuss the much-awaited trip to Disney World to play in the Pennsylvania High School Tournament. What an honor!

We suggested that he could start out early and walk to practice (approximately two miles) since he was always talking about getting more freedom. Alternatively, we suggested he ask our neighbor who had offered to take him to practice many times for a ride. We were excited that he might take the initiative to do something. Things at home were appalling. However, we did not know just how bad things really were.

When I arrived home at 4:30 P.M. on Thursday, the house looked like that in *Ferris Bueller's Day Off!* I came in to find everything in disarray and a very cocky Alistair, in his underwear, on the telephone. I told Alistair to excuse himself from the phone. When he got off the phone, I asked him why he was not at practice because this was the last big hurrah before the trip. He muttered, in his now familiar two-month-old guttural tone, "I didn't have no way to get there." I could not believe it! I said, "Alistair, we went over your options last night; don't you remember?" Annoyed by now, I said, "Tell me what they were!" Alistair just stared at me. His eyes were like reddish brown slits, and he was near the island in the kitchen. (In retrospect, I realized that he was standing next to all my cutlery tools. Praise the Lord for guardian angels!

My son looked at me with such disdain. Unfortunately, I had been very familiar with looks of intolerance for the last two years (but very noticeably the last six months) and just thought it was a teenage phase. Even more so, the last *two months* were miserable for my husband and me with Alistair. He literally told us that he did not like us. He had an intense dislike and disrespect for me, much of which he displayed when my husband was absent and I attempted to deal with alone, without involving my husband, because I knew that he would not tolerate Alistair being insolent toward me. I later discovered that absolute disregard for women was an attribute of this beast. Alistair would later refer to me as "the witness."

Two years prior, my husband saw Alistair sitting on our porch with a friend of his from the neighborhood with headphones on his ears, inquired what Alistair was listening to, and discovered that it was rap music. Alistair's dad confronted him. Alistair told his dad that he wanted to listen to rap music and do whatever he wanted to do. My husband explained the repercussions of listening to something so detrimental and explained that there are rules/standards/precepts that everyone has to live by, and no one can always do exactly what he wants to do. However, if you live a moral and righteous life in Jesus Christ, you will probably get to do many things that your heart desires because you will desire the good that God has for you and will prosper in His Word. We used the holy Scriptures of the Bible (which Alistair was very familiar with, having grown up on the Word of God) and even secular reasoning to explain that what goes in will come out, to support our case. Garbage in equals garbage out. He understood, but did not like it.

Alistair insisted that if we would just allow him to listen to the beat, he would not digest the words. Ha! Ha! We explained that not only would he digest the words, but he also would act on them. We explained that the biblical truth applies in the secular realm as well; whatever you hear enough of, you eventually will have faith enough to do! Even if it does mean having faith enough for selling your soul to the devil and being damned to an eternal hell! Ergo, there would be no rap music allowed in our home. In addition, his dad told him that he'd better not see him listening to anyone else's music. Alistair had always been a very quiet, compliant, and though gruff at times, honest and truthful child, and we never gave it another thought.

Occasionally, Alistair would raise the issue of rap music, and his dad would promptly retort that he would absolutely, unequivocally never be allowed to listen to rap music . . . at all! Being acutely aware of the pull of this world in which we live, we always kept the boys active in church youth activities, sports, martial arts, Boy Scouts and so on. We were very hands-on parents, and our sons were active children. It is not as if Alistair did not have enough stimulation. His dad would reiterate and illustrate the repercussions of listening to rap music using interesting, tangible examples. Therefore, the occasional adolescent dislike that children have for their parents did not surprise us because we raised his older brother, and we knew that there were times when he did not like us, either. Moreover, he was now sold out for the Lord. However, this was different; it was not the same.

I repeated the question and asked what his options were, and he continued to stare. I was not used to such obstinate behavior. I moved toward Alistair and told him I would "pop" him if he did not answer me. He continued to stare. Please understand this: We did not spare the rod so that the child would be spoiled. We raised our sons in the love and admonishment of the Lord, respecting them as God's wonderful gifts that they were. Each son received no more than four "real" spankings in his entire life because they were bright, pleasant, reasonable, and compliant children. Time permitting, we always explained the "whys" of everything to them and were always able to converse about the matter on a mutually respectful way. However, there were times when there was no conversation, and it was just Dad or Mom talking. This being the case, we did not tolerate disrespectful and insolent behavior. Actually, especially when they were little boys, it vexed our sons to have ever witnessed a playmate disrespect an adult because they were taught early on that it was not acceptable behavior. Our home was the "Kool-Aid house" on the block. My husband was the neighborhood Boy Scout leader, karate instructor, and young male Bible study teacher. So, you see, our boys may have answered by saying, "Yes, Mom" or "Yes, Dad" in a laborious voice and then retreated to their bedrooms and mumbled under their breath just as we do with the Lord, but they never blatantly disrespected us by not responding to a question.

This refusing to answer mode was something that we had never experienced before, and it was very unsettling. Just as I walked toward Alistair (with reddish brown slits, actually glaring like hot coals), he answered almost as if he were being directed to answer against his will, but he answered just the same.

I told Alistair to straighten up the kitchen and please get dressed because his dad would arrive shortly, and together they would attend the meeting and picnic. Alistair began to speak disrespectfully toward me, and at that time, my husband came in and asked what happened to the house and why Alistair was speaking to me that way. It seemed that Alistair had been growing progressively belligerent, particularly since he was prohibited from listening to rap music a year and a half before, but even more so over the previous six months. We had no idea that this was the day that the "jig would be up" because this time, Alistair did not transition into a convenient excuse for his tone and tenor. This time, Alistair had an attitude like, "So?" The beast had just about as much as he could take with this restraint stuff. Therefore, Alistair looked at my husband and reiterated, "I told her . . .!" My husband grabbed a saucepan, held it up, and said, "Who do you think you're talking to?" Alistair stared with those reddish brown eyes and started to speak again. I interrupted and told Alistair to iron his pants and get ready. Alistair started to answer me flippantly again, and my husband rebuked him. Alistair picked up his black jeans and black T-shirt and ironed them.

My husband and son went to the meeting and picnic, and I went for my evening walk with my neighbor. While we were walking, I told her that Alistair was truly getting out of hand and that we would continue to pray for him and seek God's will and godly counsel. When I returned to our home, I entered, and I felt very pensive. My girlfriend called on the telephone, and I shared my concerns with her. I asked her to intercede in prayer for all of us. Just as I completed my request, I heard the door open, and I told her that I would have to go because I needed to know what transpired at the meeting.

I rushed to the door to meet a perplexed husband and a very disgruntled son. I asked what was going on, and my husband remarked that Alistair had refused to sit with him at the picnic or the meeting. He alienated himself and sat away from the group. As we talked, I asked Alistair why he looked so angry. He began to speak disrespectfully toward me again, and my husband asked him if he had completely lost his mind. For a second, just for a nanosecond, our Alistair (the one we used to know before he became a recluse, a person who talked to himself—later we realized that he wasn't talking to himself, but instead rehearsing vulgar rap lyrics; a person who disrespected his parents and never smiled; a person who started performing repetitive motions as if he wasn't in control of his own body; a person who frightened the Christian psychologist that we took him to talk with until the blood left her face), yes, our Alistair came back and showed an inkling of emotion and said, "You threatened to hit me earlier!" My husband replied, "Yes, I did, Son. You cannot go around speaking to your mom and me any old kind of way. We will not have it! If you cannot comply with the rules of the house, I guess you'll just have to leave!"

(I was mortified at my husband's words. We were the perfect nuclear family, were we not? We raised our children in the admonition of the Lord. I mean, our boys' lives were charted out for success and prosperity from the womb. No, no, this was like a very bad movie! I wanted to leave the theater.)

At this point, I asked my husband if we could have a word in private, and he said yes. I told Alistair to go in the basement and wait there until we called him to come upstairs. As we went upstairs, *Alistair appeared to be going toward the basement.*

As we discussed our son in our bedroom, my husband said that we had to take extreme action. We had fasted, prayed, conversed, reasoned with him over and over again, sought medical advice, sought counseling, and more, and maybe it was time to allow him to visit a family member that he repeatedly wanted to move in with for a few days so that we could discern God's will in the matter. I agreed, and my husband left our bedroom. When my husband left the room, I felt led by the Holy Spirit to lay prostrate before the Lord and cry out to God to have mercy! "Have mercy, O God!" I said repeatedly, over and over again.

After a few minutes, I heard the disturbing sound of the planter being knocked over in the foyer. I opened the bedroom door, and as I ran down the stairs, I heard my husband shout, "Josmamie!" several times. Then, "My God, Josmamie! He stabbed me, Josmamie! Bring my gun! I'm gonna shoot him!" As I descended the stairs, I saw a knocked-over plant, blood, and a knife in the foyer. As I entered the living room, I saw my husband restraining Alistair on the couch and blood pouring from my husband's face and hands. I cried out, "O Lord, have mercy! I'm calling 911!" My husband shouted to me once again to get his gun, and he must have let up off Alistair long enough for Alistair to get loose and dash out the front door. I called 911, told them what transpired, and hung up the telephone. I attempted to help my husband, who was able to get a dishcloth to hold his face together and wrap his hands until the ambulance came. All the while, he was looking for his gun. I have never been stabbed by anyone, and I guess revenge might have been my first response as well. It was all so horrible and sudden!

My husband found his gun. As I tried to minister to my husband and calm him down and keep him from looking for a weapon, I finally confessed to him that I could not breathe and that my chest was hurting. When I told him that, he said he was sorry and handed me the gun. I took the gun, ran outside, and threw it under the car in the driveway.

The police and ambulance arrived. A little cleaned up by now, my husband was sitting on a chair in the living room, holding his face and hand. As the officers entered our home, all my husband could see were the guns that rested on their hips, he told me later. Immediately, the Holy Spirit told him that he would have to make a decision to forgive Alistair. He said immediately, all the love that he had ever known for his baby boy flooded his heart. He greeted the officers and began to say things like, "Officer, please know that the person who committed this act is really not my son. My son would not do anything like this. (The officers looked a little perplexed.) My husband went on to make a plea for Alistair's safety by saying, "And sir, you need only call him by name when you catch him. He is very compliant and will come to you. Don't pull your guns, officers; please don't hurt my baby."

As the neighbors watched from the streets and their homes, the paramedics strapped my beloved on the gurney and drove off in the ambulance to the hospital. I was told by the police officers to remain at our home until the detective arrived and interviewed me. Blood was everywhere! I prayed quietly to myself as the officer assigned to watch me followed me from room to room to assure that I didn't touch any evidence. I was clearly not in charge, and I requested that he allow me to clean up the blood so I could occupy myself. He very respectfully told me that it was evidence and not allowed. What a tragedy!

The detective arrived at our home and questioned me, took pictures and evidence, and left. A police officer was assigned to sit outside our home and keep our home under surveillance in case our son returned in the night. I showered, dressed, and drove to the hospital to be with my husband, who was being attended to by a plastic surgeon.

When I arrived at the emergency entrance, the nurses were so kind and escorted me back to my husband. When I entered the room, I could hear my husband ministering the Romans Road to salvation to the nurses who were assisting him. I was so pleased with him and so honored to be his wife.

With tears in our eyes, we embraced, and I held his uncut hand as the surgeon completed suturing forty-one stitches in his face and twenty-one stitches in his other hand. Alistair had stabbed my husband twice. The first incision was a half inch southwest of his left eye, and the second wound was inflicted a quarter of an inch from his left ear, diagonally across his cheek and down within an eighth of an inch of his mouth. During the mêlée, my husband also sustained cuts in his left hand. We received post-surgical instructions and quietly left the hospital.

We prayed before starting the car, thanked God for His faithfulness toward us as a family, and prayed for Alistair's safety. As we drove home, I asked my husband what had occurred. He said that when he descended the stairs after our discussion, he went to the basement door and told Alistair to come upstairs. He said as Alistair came up the stairs, he had a cocky smile on his face. My husband and Alistair walked toward the foyer, and my husband explained to Alistair that he would get his wish, that he could leave and stay with other family members, and we would come and get him in a few days. Then my husband said that Alistair stood at the door in a swaggering manner and said, "I ain't going nowhere without my stuff!" My husband said he was stunned because his boys had never spoken to him like that. My husband said he told Alistair to go out the door and get into the van and that he would bring his clothes to him tomorrow, but for now, he had to leave. At this, Alistair replied, "I said, 'I ain't going nowhere without my stuff!'" My husband said, "This time, I said, 'Okay, just stand there; we'll see if you're leaving or not!'"

My husband went to the laundry room and took a rubber hose off the back of the washing machine and returned to the foyer, where Alistair was standing, and once again told Alistair to go out and get into the van. Alistair refused, my husband hit Alistair on his buttocks with the hose, and

Alistair hollered. Then my husband hit Alistair with the hose again, and this time Alistair raised his hand and quickly hit my husband twice in the face (so my husband thought). When Alistair hit him, my husband slipped on the foyer rug, knocked over the plant, and landed on his back. Alistair rushed over and stood over my husband. (We found out later that when Alistair heard our bedroom door close, before going into the basement to await our call, he hid a knife in his pants, under his shirt.) When my husband saw Alistair standing over him, he grabbed Alistair by the ankles, and we believe angels supernaturally helped my husband pick him up in the air and carry him over to the sofa in the living room, and he held him down on the couch. Alistair's eyes were closed, and my husband called me as he stared down at Alistair. He felt something trickle down his face, and as he held Alistair down, he glanced in the mirror over the sofa and saw that he had been stabbed, not merely hit. He had already yelled for me, and that is when he eventually said, "My God, Josmamie! He stabbed me, Josmamie! Bring my gun! I'm gonna shoot him!" By that time, I was standing at the living room entrance.

After that explanation, we drove home in silence.

Upon arrival at our home, we noticed that the police vehicle was not in front of our door and were a little apprehensive to enter the house. We did enter and retrieved a phone message from the detective stating that Alistair had evidently fled our home and immediately went to a different township and turned himself in to police. Alistair had a one-eighth-inch scratch on his left hand and requested police to be taken to the emergency room for treatment. We immediately left the house to be with our son.

When we arrived at the emergency entrance, we sat with the receptionist, answered all applicable questions, and requested that the police officers allow us to visit with our son. We were escorted to where Alistair was being held;

he was guarded by three guards. We saw our youngest boy handcuffed and with shackles on his ankles. He looked like any other teenage boy, except this boy had no hope, and his eyes were lifeless.

My heart was broken to see my boy like this. I was numb. Yet, God was faithful, and through His grace, I was able to walk up to him and lovingly stroke and examine his hand. (Alistair had a small scratch on his hand, which they smeared a liquid coating on to protect the skin.) He showed no emotion. I told him I loved him and walked toward the door.

Next, my beloved husband walked near Alistair and said, "Hello." Alistair would not respond. In the presence of the officers surrounding Alistair, my beloved asked Alistair if he could come near to him so my husband could whisper in his ear. Alistair responded in a guttural tone, "Naw, that's i`te" (all right). My husband then stepped back and said, "Well, son, I just wanted to whisper that I love you and I forgive you." Alistair looked up at his dad with contempt in his eyes; the officers shook their heads and bowed them to their chests. We quietly left the hospital and went home and rested for three hours.

We had no idea what lay ahead as we entered the detective's office at 7 A.M. on Friday, August 24, 2001.

The detective informed us that the district attorney had decided to try Alistair as an adult for attempted murder and other charges. In addition, my husband would be charged with a misdemeanor offense. We were shocked and devastated! At worst, we thought we would attend family counseling or something and go on with life, but that was not so. Our world was about to change.

(Prior to Alistair 's backsliding, he was known as a boy who would believe God for anything! Alistair would stand on the Word of God for everything and was not ashamed of the gospel of Christ. He would never even carry a book on top of the Bible because in his opinion, "God's Word was higher than any other word." For approximately two or more years, my husband had been praying, "Lord, please bring Alistair back to his first love, the Lord Jesus Christ! Change him, Lord! Do whatever You have to do to save him!)

We left the detective's office and went to the judge to plead on Alistair 's behalf. The Lord touched the judge's heart; he had mercy on us and sent Alistair to a mental health facility for adults to be evaluated for a few days. We followed the police car and signed the admission papers. Alistair showed no remorse.

Weary and worn, my husband with stitches in face and hand, by God's grace, we returned home and changed into our work clothes to clean and paint our new church building for our first Sunday service. The Lord sustained and strengthened us to go forth with ministry in spite of the attacks of the enemy.

This gave us time to seek God's perfect will and provision for our Alistair 's destiny. In our hearts, Alistair was coming out of this situation as pure gold! O Lord, have mercy!

Chapter 3

Post-Incident

On Saturday, August 25, 2001, we had to pack some clothes to take to Alistair at the mental facility and discovered some very disturbing elements in his room. Thinking back, that should have been a red flag. We recently moved to a new home and asked Alistair how he would like his room decorated. He requested that we paint his room black with black carpet, a black spread, black blinds and a black ceiling fan. We knew teenagers are "different" people and told him that there was no contrast and that we would compromise with him. His color scheme would be black and white with hints of gold to break the monotony. Alistair was always an extremely neat person and always kept his room in order. We, therefore, hardly ever went through his things because at first glance, every drawer, closet, and storage chest was in order. His older brother was not as neat, so we were always sifting through his things in an effort to straighten up his room and to discern what was going on in his life. However, we did not exercise this parental prerogative with Alistair as much because he was so orderly and compliant.

Parents, it is your parental prerogative to go through your child's possessions without permission. You are your child's guardian and guide. You are working in

concert with the Holy Spirit of God to get him or her to the other side. Do not be complacent. You must be cognizant of your child's affairs, friends, and whereabouts. It is your prerogative and duty to God and your child. Do not hand him or her over to the devil without a fight. Stand your ground. Many criminals lament that they lacked parental guidance and discipline. Not only do children need it; they want it!

During the summer of 2001, Alistair worked with my husband. In an effort to teach responsibility, it was decided that Alistair would use his earnings to purchase his back-to-school clothes for the fall. However, while visiting family when my husband and I went away for a weekend, Alistair requested they take him to the mall so that he could buy a portable CD player. My husband shared with family that Alistair was insolent and becoming very hard to deal with and that under no circumstances was he to watch any inappropriate movies or TV shows, or listen to any music, with the exception of spiritual music, which edified the Lord. This was not an unusual request for our sons. On occasion, while they visited family members' homes, they would tell family members that they needed to be excused because they were not allowed to participate in certain activities. Therefore, this request was just a reminder, but nothing new. Family and friends may not, and bureaucracy definitely will not, understand spiritual matters. Family members often are loving and caring people; nevertheless, they still don't understand. Family retorted, "Kids will be kids," and, "We were not perfect teenagers, so don't be so hard!" Beloved, when family and friends do not understand spiritual matters, your talking will be ignored. It will be as if you are speaking "Martian" to them because they do not speak your language.

Family members took Alistair to the store, and he bought a CD player with his earnings. We did not know that Alistair had it. We also later discovered that he requested family members take him to a sound shop, where he purchased five explicit gangsta rap CDs.

As my husband emptied Alistair's gym bag, he found five gangsta rap CDs and the CD player. Alistair was not concerned about clothes; he needed "his stuff." It—the demon influencing Alistair—needed to feed that hellish music, which took Alistair's very soul. We found out later that the reason that the last two months were so hellish in our home was because Alistair would digest the music with headphones all day at summer football practice and then retire to bed early, close and lock his door, and go to sleep listening to that music all night. Alistair was saturating himself with demonic lyrics twenty-four hours a day for two months, except when we made him attend church with us on Sundays and weekly Bible studies. Yes, beloved, the devil absolutely attends church! Like the demon-possessed man in Luke 8 who abode in the tombs, the enemy of our souls had a trophy, and he was not trying to give him up! Alistair's mind was like mush!

We would later hear in Alistair's testimony that he continued to sneak and listen to rap music and be fueled by the demonic/hate/dehumanizing lyrics from the time he was in fifth grade when his father first chastised him about it until that tragic night three years later when the devil could not stay under wraps any longer.

Not only did my husband find the devil's music; he also found several crudely formed razor and pencil ensembles tucked under neatly folded linens in Alistair's storage chests. There were three of them. We can only assume whom they were for.

Chapter 4

God's Son

On Sunday, August 20, 2000, approximately one year before this incident, I began to keep a log on Alistair, primarily because his behavior was getting more defiant and he seemed to be resisting the things of God. Journaling comforted me, and I knew deep in my spirit that one day, I would stand back and rejoice in the deliverance of my son. God has such precious ways of preparing and protecting us, even when it looks like we have gone down for the count.

The journal starts with:

"And this is Alistair's victory, which has overcome the world! It is His salvation! Glory to God forevermore! Our God loves us all so much that He gave His only begotten Son to die for our sins; thank You, Lord! 'For God so loved the world, that he gave his only begotten Son, that whosoever believeth in him should not perish, but have everlasting life' (John 3:16). This logbook is dedicated to my Alistair. my baby, who hears. When Leah named her son, she said that God heard her. Alistair's name is so appropriate because I cried out to the Lord to spare Alistair's life. Many babies died during the time that he was to be born. The Lord almighty heard me. Thank You, Lord!

"I love my two sons so very much! I remember when Son I (affectionate name for our oldest son) was born. I told him, 'I like you so much! You have such a pleasant personality, little boy!' And I remember when my Alistair was born; I looked into his quiet brown eyes and said, 'I love you.' I loved both of them from the womb. Praises be to God!"

I continued to write. "The Lord has led me to log some things about Alistair 's adolescence. So much is happening. We are all very challenged by his sullen attitude and his disrespectful and selfish ways. His dislike and intolerance for me astound me sometimes! But look at God!

"This journal will tell of God's grace, mercy, and faithfulness unto us. God is delivering us all as I write. We are going to pray the solutions, not the problems. We commit Alistair to the Most High God! The God of David. The great I AM. Here Lord. We dedicate the young great end-time warrior to You. Thank You, Lord!"

Each entry in the logbook tells of God's faithfulness in the midst of perceived adolescent chaos. God is so long-suffering with us and interested in our salvation that He will go to any length to reach humankind and express His love for us — even death on a cross, even granting a boy his wish for his dying dog.

Log Entry: Friday, August 25, 2000

Alistair is facing a difficult situation in his life. Sandy is very sick and must be put down. Alistair said we are willing to kill her. (He will not call it putting her down; Alistair said that it is murder.) Alistair proclaimed, "Why can't she just lie down in her yard and die with dignity?" With that, he walked out of the room and went into the yard to feed Sandy and play with her. He came in later and went to sleep. We're praying for God's mercy and grace.

Log Entry: Saturday, August 26, 2000

It was early in the morning, and I heard my husband whisper for me to come to the window and look down. He was in the yard with Sandy, and she seemed to be peaceably asleep, but she was not. She had died in her yard during the night with dignity. From Alistair 's mouth to God's ears, Alistair 's words were heard, and in grace and mercy, God gave him the desires of his heart.

Change of Environment

We moved from the inner city to the suburbs on September 1, 2000. Initially, the change seemed to be great for Alistair. He had more freedom than what he had experienced in the inner city. Although he had been reared in a beautiful inner city neighborhood with beautiful homes and pleasant people, it was still "the city." And Alistair and his brother were not allowed to do everything and go everywhere.

(We would later find out that Alistair's secret life started in the city and continued to a more "sophisticated" level once we moved to the suburbs.) In our new neighborhood, Alistair had the liberty to catch the yellow school bus and stay after school for afternoon activities. Being a natural athlete and being from the city, he could play football and "yard" ball very well and became an instant asset to his new suburban team. However, with this new freedom, we noticed Alistair becoming even more distant toward us, and his tolerance for anyone who was not "cool" was appalling. We continued to pray and seek God's face in the matter, and the Lord continued to tell us to pray the solution and not the problem. We continued to pray and reach out ever the more to our son.

School Altercation

On January 8, 2001, we received a call from the vice principal of Alistair's middle school, and she informed me that Alistair and another young man had an altercation. She said that Alistair had assaulted the young man; I immediately inquired if the young man was all right and extended my condolences. (I later found out from Alistair that when the vice principal ended our phone conversation, she told him that his parents seemed to be decent, caring people, and only because of the phone conversation would she not request he be taken in to police custody, but would allow his father to take him in for interrogation later that evening when he arrived home from work.)

The argument was about Alistair's calculator. The boy picked up Alistair's calculator off the desk, and Alistair requested he put it down. The boy continued to horse around with the calculator, and Alistair continued to ask him to put it down. Finally, the boy put it down, and Alistair told him that he would repay him for what he had done. The boy became concerned and told Alistair that he was only kidding around and that he was sorry for what he had done. Alistair told him that was not acceptable, and when they were dismissed from class, Alistair walked behind the boy and smacked him in the back of his head. The boy turned around, and the fight ensued.

After Columbine, most schools revamped their no violence/tolerance policies. The police interrogated both Alistair and the boy independently. After hearing both sides of the story, both sets of parents were fined $165.50 for the altercation, and the boys were made to attend conflict resolution sessions together. My husband expressed that he didn't feel that the other boy and his parents should have been fined and expressed that to police officers. A police officer looked at him as if he were strange.

We knew that Alistair's reaction was maniacal, but we knew that nothing was too hard for GOD, and that God was not in heaven wringing His hands, wondering what to do. We continued to stay focused on the Lord and trust HIM for the results. Below are red flags that were realized in retrospect.

Red Flags

1. Wickedness: Complete disregard for the things of GOD.
2. Disdain for parents.
3. No joy. Happiness concerns what is happening now; joy is eternal.
4. Lack of purpose and goals.
5. Wearing dark clothes.
6. Reclusive behavior.
7. Unwholesome relationships or no friends at all.
8. Delight in causing or viewing pain inflicted on others.
9. Drugs or other intoxicants, sex, and rock 'n' roll.
10. Falling grades in school; lack of concentration.

Log Entry: Saturday, February 3, 2001

This morning, I went into my son's room to kiss him awake. It was something I often did in the mornings before leaving for work. I bent down to kiss Alistair, and he literally jumped out of the bed, and looking just like a demon, said, "Don't touch me! Why did you have to do that? Naw, Naw! Don't do that!" I was devastated and said, "Alistair, don't say that; you don't mean that." I left Alistair's bedroom and entered our room. I tried to silence my crying with a towel up to my mouth in the bathroom, but my husband could hear me. Being a man of action, he went into Alistair's room and asked him if he would like to leave, leave his clothes here and go, perhaps to an area back in the city. He would have a week to decide.

Pamela, Ina, Donna, Lillie, and Lisa have been praying. Lillie sent a list of prayers to be prayed for rebellious teenagers. Donna said that he is wrestling. Nana "really got with him!" Auntie wrote a letter of encouragement. We all believe God.

Alistair remains distant; there is a perceived reconciliation. He is watching his attitude because he likes his environment and does not want to be put out. Also, girls are interested in him, per one of his teachers. They are at his locker all the time. We thought it was nice that he liked someone.

Little did we know that our quiet son had been sexually active since seventh grade. He would later tell us that our allowing him to join the basketball team gave him one hour of free time until we arrived to encourage him in the games. We kept our children very close and could always account for their time. Evidently, a fellow seventh-grade girl invited him to her home between class and the game and introduced him to sex and marijuana. Alistair never wanted us to come up to school for his games, and we thought it was because he was shy. One day, I noticed his eyes were red and immediately carted him off to the doctor. The doctor examined him and told me that he suffered from sinusitis. Who knew?

We were Christians, right? We did all the right things. We raised our boys up in the admonition and real life application of the Word of God. They knew that the devil sought to steal, kill, and destroy the children of God. They knew that life and death were in the power of the tongue and that we always had to choose life rather than death. They knew that out of the heart of man, the mouth speaks. They knew, didn't they? Why did he choose death as opposed to life? Why did he choose to rebel?

We need guidance from the Lord. He alone can help us. Amen.

Log Entry: Monday, February 12, 2001

The WORD works! Hallelujah! We praise God for His faithfulness and how He loves us so! We have been praying prayers for rebellious teens over Alistair, and last night, the Lord told me that I had been strengthened and to get up from under that tree! (He is so wonderful.) I was to release Pamela and to get busy myself. I thank God! Today the Holy Spirit had me buy a bottle of pure virgin olive oil. The Lord led me exactly where to go, and I got it for $1.20, which is unheard of for this particular brand. Glory to God! I had anointed Alistair's room before, but God wanted a *fresh* anointing. I came home, prayed, and anointed Alistair 's room. I know our heavenly Father is working this thing out! Thank You, Lord! Oh, how we love You! The Lord spoke to my spirit, "I have saved Alistair's life for such a time as this." I was also reminded of what Pam said to me, and I pondered these things. The Lord is good, my Shield, my Strength in time of need.

Log Entry: Sunday, February 25, 2001

My God is perfect in all His ways! God reminded me that it is not about me!

Me: "Lord, What do I need to learn from this situation with Alistair?"

God: "Grace, which abounds."

Me: "Show me what to confess, Lord, and I will confess it! I am hurt, bewildered, and, quite frankly, tired of all the warfare. Tell me what to do, Lord, and I will do it!"

God: "Stand."

Me: "Lord, that is what we are called to do. You empower us by the power of the Holy Spirit to do it for others; please help us to do it for ourselves!"

God: "Stand."

Me: "Lord, *Alistair* means 'to hear.'"

Me: "Lord, please give Alistair wisdom to repent and turn from his wickedness. Lord, all that we knew to do, we did. Have mercy on us, Lord!"

God: "I have."

Me: "Lord, please help us to believe and receive Your promises."

God: "Pray the Word, which is My solution."

Log Entry: Monday, March 19, 2001

I got a call from Mrs. Harmon, Alistair's Spanish tutor. He's not completing assignments, is not organized, and is bringing the wrong books or not bringing any books at all.

We spoke to Alistair about his lack of commitment concerning his studies and threatened to take sports away from him should he not get back in line. We continually speak with our son; we pray for and pray with our Alistair. In addition, God moved on my beloved's heart to preach Proverbs (a letter from a father to his son) to Alistair. The boys grew up having family devotion and individual devotion time. However, their dad said that he wanted to step it up a notch and have one-on-one Bible study every day with Alistair.

Several years ago, I told Alistair that God laid it upon my heart to tell him that God would make Alistair wise if he would read a chapter of Proverbs each day.

No matter what it looks like, we have the victory! Hallelujah!

Prayer: A prayer of thanksgiving and a song titled "You Are My God!"

Log Entry: Saturday, April 7, 2001

This miracle is in process! Glory to God!

They grew up with family devotions; he knows how to connect with God.

The Lord is speaking to my beloved: "You've prayed. Now it is time to do. Sit down each night and systematically teach Alistair the Word of God again. I will train you as you train him. You have prayed enough. Now do it! This miracle is in process."

Log Entry: Monday, April 9, 2001

I am traveling.

My telephone rang while riding on the train; it was my beloved. He informed me that our Alistair had been suspended again. It was an incident about his shoes.

We are very troubled about Alistair. His behavior is out of control and aggressive. Systematic study came to mind again.

This morning, Chuck Swindoll was teaching on Eli's improper handling of his two sons. God would not tolerate their lack of reverence for His holiness. It confirmed for me that Alistair absolutely needed to be "checked"! God has been so merciful to us! God is warning us that Alistair is quickly heading toward self-destruction and perhaps trying to destruct us as a family along with him. However, through God's grace and mercy, God is giving us opportunity to turn this thing around. Thank You, Lord!

Prayer: Lord, please teach us the lessons and instructions that You have for us to grasp during this trial. Our prayer is that we seek Your face for instruction to come out victorious and give You all the glory!

The Lord: His salvation is nigh. His father has to follow his plan. I have placed great decision-making skills in the man of God! Turn off that television and come aside with Me. Everything I ask you to do, son, has a plan associated with it.

God: "Bring your notebook with you and write the vision. Amen."

Prayer: We want to do what You say to do, Lord.

Log Entry: Monday, April 23, 2001

Alistair is God's son!

Alistair and Donnie (our godson) traveled to visit our oldest son this weekend, and it was a blessed trip. They took the train, and it was an experience for them. I pray and I know that God met them there!

A vision: I see Alistair and Son I ministering together!

I thank God for Alistair's, our neighbors', and all our loved ones' salvation, in Jesus' name.

Log Entry: Sunday, May 13, 2001

I prayed for God's forgiveness. I cried out to God for the pain of the day. I was disappointed by the perceived lack of homage expressed toward *me* today. Wow! No gifts or cards from my children, no "Happy Mother's Day," no anything!

I asked Alistair for a happy Mother's Day smile, and he said, "I'm eating." He never acknowledged me! Glory be to God! No cards or acknowledgments from anyone. I cried out to the Lord, and He started talking to me about ministry!

He started telling me that I was not instrument-rated. He reminded me that all my expectations come from Him! He told me to be grateful that I had hair to roll, hands to work, and eyes to see! He told me that even though they did not say, "Happy Mother's Day" to me, I still had the following:

- A husband who loves God, me, and his sons.
- A son who loves God and his family.
- A son who will love God one day, will stand by himself if necessary, and knows God's Word.

I repented because I am blessed and should not behave like a big baby! Not even a baby Christian; just a baby!

God reminded me that I am a Proverbs 31 woman, in Jesus' name!

Glory to God! I receive it, in Jesus' name!

The Lord told me He was stripping me.

God reminded me of how our Lord Jesus was stripped on the cross.

God said He was stripping me to be strengthened!

I cannot go on if I do not become instrument-rated!

The Lord wants me to be strengthened in His Word so that I will be instrument-rated!

I am blessed, so very blessed!

Thank You, Lord!

God: "Will you be Jesus in Alistair's life?"

In service today, the Lord showed me that my husband was God, Son I was the Holy Spirit, and I was Jesus in Alistair's life.

God wanted an answer to "Will you be Jesus in Alistair's life?"

Wow! My spirit felt a drawing, a pulling on it.

I got a minuscule glimpse of what my Savior endured. The Lord said I had to allow myself to be **stripped** so that I could be **strengthened** to go the places to do the **exploits** that we are to accomplish in Christ Jesus! Hallelujah!

God told me such a sweet, sweet, encouraging word to sustain me as we go on . . . .

"Don't faint, Josmamie! Remember that a Christlike example is the greatest gift parents can give their children."

Log Entry: Saturday, July 28, 2001

"Oh, how I love Jesus because He first loved me!" It is really bad!

I spoke to a Christian counselor at New Life Live about Alistair yesterday, and the counselor gave me several leads on how we may want and need to proceed. Again, as we have asked so many times in the past, I said, "God, what should we do?"

God said, "Pray the solution." I prayed the following: for a child's future, against unwholesome relationships, against drugs and other intoxicants, against sexual perversion, and against lack of purpose and goals. Ironically, I did not know why God would have me pray all of the above because as far as I knew, my son was not doing any of those things. He was a teenager going through some tumultuous emotions, but he was basically a nice kid, right?

We would later discover these things:

Unwholesome relationships. Alistair met children from another school district, and together they would wait until dusk (in the winter when it gets dark earlier), and between school ending and evening basketball games beginning, they would hide in the bushes, hold up other children, and take their money. My husband and I would arrive at the games and root Alistair on. The children never knew it was Alistair; it was dark. And the very people that Alistair stole from at night, he broke bread with during the day. Beloveds, he was not the brains behind the stickups, but he was a willing participant.

Drugs and other intoxicants. Much later, we discovered that Alistair had a healthy drug habit. We never suspected anything because it only seemed that the "sinus" problem happened during sinus season. We always laid money down ever since they were little and never missed any money. Alistair did not steal from us, but he did steal from his classmates. In retrospect, we realize that we constantly bought batteries, but could never find them. He stole our batteries (out of the drawers, appliances, and so on) so that he could listen to his CD and have hellish music at all times.

Sexual perversion. If his ninth-grade teacher had not told us that girls were interested in him, we would have never known that Alistair even acknowledged that girls existed. His dad had talks with the boys about their sexuality since they were young enough to understand and ask questions. However, we would later find out that when Alistair was in seventh grade, a girl approached him about going home with her between the end of the school day and basketball practice and games to smoke marijuana and have sex. We had no idea! Alistair was never a very huggy-kissy child, but he had given me a hug and a kiss every day. In retrospect, I realize that it was around that time that he stopped letting me touch him. He would allow other female family members to touch him, but not me. I can only gather that it was that he knew women carnally, and he was ashamed.

Lack of purpose and goals. We would ask Alistair what he wanted to be when he grew up, and he would reply that he would move out West, get a dog and a wolf, live alone forever, and go into town when necessary to get food. Before he and his brother were born, while they kicked in the womb, we spoke words of prosperity over their lives. We preached Philippians 4:13 and 4:19 to them every day in word, precept, and action. Why was he so withdrawn? Why did he have unnatural affections toward me? I did not have a clue; I thought it was all a phase.

There was a big blowup between his dad and Alistair last night. I repent for my prideful ways; I did not want people to know what we were going through. My husband joined the Bible study with tears in his eyes and asked the saints to pray. He told them that Alistair wanted nothing to do with God, and that it was breaking his heart. The people rallied around us and prayed. I praised God for the release!

We received prayer for our direction as parents and prayer for my beloved, for wisdom as a pastor and dad.

Log Entry: Sunday, July 29, 2001

Alistair's dad decided that we would not attend the family reunion. There have been more words between Alistair's dad and Alistair. I am praying for reconciliation. In church today, the pastor made an interesting point: "Even as teenagers we have wisdom. At that point in our lives, wisdom is called *parents*. God gives us wisdom/parents to tell the young about pitfalls and the dangers of wrong decisions that we make in life. It is to our advantage to heed what wisdom says because it will spare us pain and sorrow when we're young and when we're old." For a moment, I looked over at Alistair, and Alistair was listening attentively. Then, just like something took over, he lowered his head and seemed forlorn.

ACTION ITEMS: Read to Alistair, dictate to Alistair (have him write the sentences I dictate, then use William Strunk and E.B. White's book *The Elements of Style* to edit punctuation), and have him practice typing.

Log Entry: Saturday, August 11, 2001

We will all bow one day before the throne of Jesus! Hallelujah! Glory to God for what He is doing! God is about to turn this thing around! Glory! Glory!

Recap: Last week when Alistair visited family, they allowed him to buy or bought him a CD player and CD. The CD was vulgar. My beloved went into Alistair's room one morning (actually, the door had to be unlocked with a key) and saw the set. He played the set and found it to be vulgar. (God did not leave us ignorant.) To prove a point, my husband took the CD to our family, and they exclaimed, "We all did stuff. I don't care as long as he doesn't play it where I can hear," etc. It was a devastating blow to my husband because he needed their support.

He feels that that encounter lost us ground because now he has an adult defending Alistair's stand, going against my husband's authority position as Alistair's father. He is so hurt and overwhelmed. Alistair is angry because my beloved took the CD and left it at our family member's home. He is so angry that he has not spoken to us since the date of the incident . . . . But God!

The promises of God are *yeah* and *amen* in Christ Jesus. Bless Your name, dear Lord!

Chapter 5

Claiming Victory
(After the Attack)

Log Entry: Sunday, August 26, 2001

This is our victory which overcometh the world, even our faith! Hallelujah!

Our Alistair is coming out of this situation as pure gold! The Lord is so merciful to us!

Recap: On each occasion that I have spoken to my son, I have told him how much we love him and miss him. We had to inform his football coach, the teachers, and others of Alistair's status. God is doing an awesome work right in the midst of the chaos and pain. We glorify the Lord! It is interesting, although Alistair is still very arrogant, it seems as though he is still willing to speak to me on the telephone. It could just be the mother in me/my flesh that longs to be accepted by my son, and I thank God that one day Alistair will learn what LOVE is and that he is truly loved and valued.

Throughout each conversation, I tell him that I love and miss him, and he does not reply. However, it is not about me! It is about doing the perfect will of God! Hallelujah! Evangelist Brandt prophesized that Alistair needs to come to the end of himself. I know it is true. However, all the time, I cry out, "Have mercy, O Lord! Have Mercy!"

Today we contacted several people concerning Alistair's situation:

1. Shelly (the social worker)
2. Mr. Bob Hillman (the intervention person)
3. Anchor Academy for Boys in Montana
4. Mr. Lofty at New Life Youth and Family Services
5. Mr. George Berman for lawyer referrals

I long to hold my baby in my arms and tell him that I love him. His dad cannot seem to stop crying. I cry at the drop of a hat too. There are so many dynamics going on, but there is ONE GOD! One Jehovah Shalom! One Savior! Thank You, Lord!

Alistair loves his parents, in Jesus' name! Praise be to God, from whom all blessings flow!

Log Entry: Tuesday, August 28, 2001

The Lord is sovereign. Praise be to God! The Lord has done a mighty thing! Today, my beloved cleaned the house. Yesterday evening, as we packed Alistair's bag to take him some clothes, we found five explicit gangsta rap CDs hidden in his Nike bag. We also found a very expensive CD player; my husband found the receipt for it today.

My husband listened to the tapes that we found and said that each one contained horrific lyrics about raping, killing, and other frightening topics.

As my husband surveyed Alistair's room, he found three or four razors and a knife wrapped within pencils and black tape. My husband cleaned every stitch of Alistair's clothing as well as his room, and threw out everything that would not bow down to the lordship of Christ. We prayed and anointed the room, and my husband turned Alistair's radio to WFIL AM (560), the Christian station. It stays on twenty-four hours per day. When you walk into Alistair's room, it is now a peaceful place. God did not leave us ignorant, and we praise Him for it.

The church came over to our home and ministered to us in an awesome way! We thank God for Alistair's deliverance and delightfulness! Glory to God!

Log Entry: Wednesday, August 29, 2001

This is the day that the Lord has made. We shall rejoice and be glad in it!

We are experiencing the mercy of God! This morning at 9:15, we went to the facility for mentally challenged adults for Alistair's hearing. God moved in a mighty way!

Alistair's doctor, Dr. Shatner, diagnosed that Alistair was "disconnected" and needed further care. Dr. Shatner told Alistair that he was going to suggest to the judge that Alistair not go to jail but to an adolescent facility if Alistair was willing to agree with him. Glory to God! Alistair agreed! And if that was not awesome enough, God moved on the detective's heart to agree with the doctor's prognosis. In other words, if the police department had not agreed with the doctor, by default, Alistair would have gone to an adult prison until trial.

God gave Alistair favor with the police! Hallelujah!

I regret that our conversations with our Alistair have not been tasteful. Alistair has started to curse. (I would later discover that Alistair had been cursing since fifth grade, when he started listening to rap music, but I never heard him.) The demon who is influencing Alistair is vile. But glory be to God! I see the Spirit of God rising up from Alistair's little toe! Ha ha! Watch the Spirit of God. Hallelujah! God's gonna turn this thing around! Amen! Amen! Amen! We praise You, O Lord!

God is working out His perfect will to His glory!
Thank You, Lord!

Log Entry: Thursday, August 30, 2001

God's mercy prevails!

Although everyone agreed, the HMO would not sanction Alistair's transfer to the Shetland hospital for mentally challenged youths.

We contacted the saints, they prayed, God answered, and glory to God, they found a bed, and my Alistair was transferred! Glory to God!

God is watching over our son!

Log Entry: Friday, August 31, 2001

Our God is mighty!

At 2:30 P.M., I met with the social worker, Ms. Phyllis, and intern doctor, Keith. Alistair refused to see me, but was glad that I brought clothes. I wrote a point paper for the doctors, a chronicle of Alistair's life so that they could know my Alistair. It ministered to me to be able to remember my sweet son.

What I chose not to include in the point paper was Alistair's threat to kill all three of us at Christmastime 2000. Alistair had told his brother that his intentions were to kill one or all three of us.

God is so merciful to have restrained the enemy as long as He did. Thank You, Lord!

Log Entry: Sunday, September 2, 2001

My hope is in Thee.

Log Entry: Wednesday, September 5, 2001

It's jubilee! God is doing a restoration work in our son's life, in Jesus' name! Hallelujah! Glory to God!

Although we have not heard from the district attorney's office, by faith, today we furthered plans to send our baby to Montana. We received the package from the Anchor Academy for Boys, and it is thorough. My beloved contacted a courier service, and representatives there estimated that they could transport Alistair to the Anchor for $5,500. Glory to God! Lord, where will the money come from?

(Most parents accompany the children to the Anchor; however, Alistair is considered extremely dangerous, and we are not allowed to escort him alone. With the other son in college, we were not prepared for this expense, but God knows all about it, so we rest in His provision.)

I got on the Web and told the saints to pray for more days from Keystone HMO so that we could get Alistair situated and make provisions for his transportation. We spoke to Donna and Bert. Bert (a retired marine) and his friend (a boxer's bodyguard) were willing to escort my husband and Alistair to Montana. They were willing to lend us money and use whatever transportation necessary to get him there.

God is so wonderful! He just wanted to encourage us with using these sweet saints of God.

This evening, we listened to the messages and heard that Detective Heap had spoken to the district attorney, and he is not sold on what we would like to do (i.e., send Alistair away to a boys boarding school in lieu of sending him locally to a Pennsylvania correctional institution for boys).

Our God is our Shield and Buckler! No good thing will He withhold from us! Glory! Glory!

We are praying, and we have energized the saints to pray that as the DA's heart is in the Lord's hand and just as the rivers of water, God will turn the DA's heart whithersoever He will. Glory! Glory!

God's got it! Thank You, Lord!

Alistair is calling people and spreading dissension. People are upset (and not understanding spiritual warfare; they are listening instead of getting clarity and praying for God to reveal the truth). Our prayer is for God's peace to comfort them and that through God's mercy, we will come on one accord during God's healing season for our dearest Alistair! In Jesus' name, we thank You and pray. Amen.

Log Entry: Thursday, September 6, 2001

On our way to speak to Portia and Dr. Keith, we received a cell call from Detective Charles Heap. Detective Heap said that the DA did not want Alistair to go to his family's. In the interim, Detective Heap was aware that we were securing a place for Alistair at the Anchor Academy for Boys.

We went to the Shetland clinic and spoke with Portia and Dr. Keith. Alistair also eventually came in.

The conversation with Portia and Dr. Keith was sobering: Alistair had equated us to pit bulls; they can be as sweet as pie and then "jump on you!"

My husband explained that there were just some things that would never be allowed in our home—not now or ever!

Alistair would not dialogue with us.

I do feel that he "listened" to me for just a minute as he was exiting out the door. Just for a moment, my Alistair was there . . . .

We returned home and arranged to have a courier/detectives transport Alistair to Montana on separate planes and arranged car reservations for my husband to get to Montana.

Since we were not allowed to travel with Alistair, my husband would have to travel several days ahead of Alistair to assure proper registration for him at the Anchor Academy for Boys.

By faith, believing that the judge would release Alistair and not send him to adult prison and would allow him to go to the Anchor, we went to Walmart and bought clothing and supplies for Alistair's year at the Anchor.

We came home tired, but in peace, knowing that Alistair would be adjudicated as a juvenile on Friday.

Log Entry: Friday, September 7, 2001

Glory to God! This is the day of Alistair's hearing! We sang an encouraging tune, believing God will turn this all around.

This morning, we arose, and I went to several credit unions to get money. God is so awesome! Where will it come from, Lord?

We needed:
- A $3,500 retainer for retired Detective Tufo.
- $1,030 for the first month's tuition.
- $1,990 for my husband's plane ticket.
- $50 for my husband's car rental.
- $85 for my husband's pocket money.

God gave us:
- $300 that we had saved in Alistair's savings account.
- $1,363 that we saved in a CD for Alistair.
- $120 from our holiday club.
- $120 from our vacation club.

This gave us $1,903. Glory to God! We needed $1,957. This was just right for God!

We had a life savings of $3,500, and we had saved saving bonds for Alistair's college education that we had in a safe deposit box.

Lord, we will cash everything in! Thank You, Lord, for the provision!

We met Detectives Moe Ellulio and Fubu at the judge's chambers and gave them Alistair's luggage and all particulars. Alistair and Detective Heap and the others arrived.

Alistair was in handcuffs and shackles.

When the judge asked Alistair if he wanted to waive the hearing, Alistair said, "I want to go to my family's."

Alistair continued to repeat what he wanted: "I want to go to my family's."

The judge realized that Alistair did not understand the question and motioned for a court-appointed attorney.

The attorney came and conferred with Alistair.

In the interim, however, the DA's office called and said that they wanted a formal hearing to determine if Alistair should be tried as an adult.

They further stated that they wanted to review the case and have the hearing on Tuesday, September 11, 2001. In addition, they wanted him taken to an adult facility and held there for the weekend.

I almost fainted! I could not catch my breath! I could not comprehend my boy entering a jail with hardened criminals, rapists and murderers! That's not a place for a well-raised Christian boy! O God, have mercy! Please, Lord, have mercy!

It was like a horror movie saga!

I started to lose it, but the Lord kept me under. They took our son to Birdville County Prison, just beyond Norristown, Pennsylvania.

Alistair is still not aware of the seriousness of everything that is going on. Our prayer: that the DA will cancel/drop the charges and we can have Alistair transported to the Anchor Academy for Boys in Montana.

Question to God: Why didn't the Lord stay the DA's hand and release Alistair to juvenile court? Why didn't God have them drop the charges and let him go?

God's answer: "I AM manifesting My perfect will in Alistair's life."

The Lord said, "This time next year, all will have a different testimony about Alistair; trust Me."

The Lord told me, "I am making Alistair a "whole man."

The commentary in my open Bible said: not a refreshed/refurbished old model, but instead a brand spanking new model! God is a "new" God! Glory! Glory!

The vision I see for Alistair: Before he shares the Word, he will say to the congregation, "I would like to minister in song unto the LORD. God looked beyond my faults and saw my needs."

My loving family is so distraught!

Lord, have mercy! Have mercy!

I love them so!

Peachie (a sister in the Lord) said something very interesting tonight:

1. Demons hate anything that is holy.
2. GOD declared that our home is a holy home.
3. No unholy coveting will be tolerated.
4. The enemy is attacking children.
   Remember the dirty caged bird story:
   Catch them.
   Play with them. (Sin is good for a season.)
   Taunt them.
   Kill them.

Alistair has a sound mind, and he will not die! I declare it in Jesus' name! Glory to GOD!

Nothing but the blood of Jesus will set our son free!

Peachie said something else that was very interesting:
Secular psychologists want to rehearse the past. Biblical counselors want to recognize that sin has taken place and the person can get better in Christ Jesus!

Glory to the Lamb!

Our son will be well in Christ Jesus!

We owe the detectives an additional $750 for yesterday's inconvenience. We had them present at the courthouse so that as soon as Alistair was acquitted, he would be swept off into their van and on his way to the academy. Since they, too, had to wait for sentencing and discharge, we were charged for three hours' inconvenience. Where will it come from, Lord? They are still holding our $3,500 retainer check.

Log Entry: Saturday, September 8, 2001

Praise the name of JESUS! Praise GOD'S holy name!

During the "waiting" yesterday, my husband and I started to sing many songs that brought us great comfort.

Then they came in and told us the things above. I was looking out the window, and this Scripture came to me: "Trust in the LORD with all thine heart; and lean not unto thine own understanding. In all thy ways acknowledge him, and he shall direct thy paths" (Proverbs 3:5-6).

God has a covenant with our family!

I told my beloved that getting up in the morning is sometimes "different" because of the uncertainty. I was just being visceral, and he explained to me that I was a parent, and GOD gave us a "protective" spirit just like His Spirit. However, God will not violate our wills. We are still asking the Lord for His perfect will. Lord, have mercy!

Log Entry: Saturday afternoon, September 8, 2001

My husband went to the church today to spruce up and paint. While my husband was at the church, Bob, the owner of the building, came by to tell him that an article on Friday's happenings was in the newspaper (front page).

When my husband returned home to let me know what had transpired, he was concerned how I would handle it. He read the article to me, and it was something to see your life in print for the whole world to observe.

However, our God knew about this from His making the foundations of the world, and it was allowed to be on the front page. God is moving by His Spirit, and we are blessed! The Word says in Acts 5:41, Peter and the apostles felt this way "and they departed from the presence of the council, rejoicing that they were counted worthy to suffer shame for his name."

After that blow, we gathered ourselves together and ran errands, including going to the supermarket to buy groceries, that I might cook dinner . . . for the first time in three weeks.

We called the prison to see how Alistair was doing. He was watching TV in an area all by himself. Look at God! The Lord had the authorities place Alistair in a separate area in an adult facility. Praise You, Lord!

This experience has taught us that we must always seek God's face and perfect will for our lives. The Lord encouraged me to call Alistair's Spanish tutor and his football coach to request they write letters of support for Alistair that we will take to the district attorney's office. God's favor is more precious than gold!

We are praying for:

- The judge.
- The lawyer (charges are aggravated assault, prohibited offensive weapons, simple assault, and reckless endangerment).

- The DA's staff.

I must contact the Birdville County Prison social worker to inquire about calls and visitations.

We praise GOD for HIS perfect will. Thank You, LORD!

Log Entry: Sunday, September 9, 2001

Letters and calls today:
- Roy Fitzgerald (football coach)
- Mrs. Christine Gore (Spanish tutor)
- Mrs. Veronica Smith (grandmother)
- Joseph Petty (football coach)
- Ret. Gen. Brill George (commissioner for Montgomery County)
- Nancy Bolden (neighbor)
- Pastor Jerry Smalley (educational advisor at Son I's college)
- Rev. and Mrs. Reggie North
- Mr. Pleasant (middle school teacher)

Log Entry: Monday, September 10, 2001

Look at the LORD!

GOD has turned the "king's heart!" Glory, Glory!

Many letters have gone forth. Uncle Butch made many calls! Look at the Lord!

We have letters from Roy Fitzgerald, Mrs. Christine Gore, Joseph Petty, and more.

My beloved went to the DA's office and met with Supervisor Nancy Longman, who behaved as if she were Alistair's lawyer instead of his accuser! Look at God!

God touched everyone's heart in the DA's office. It was awesome!

Mr. Michael Bertucci called and told us to have Alistair agree with the charges and say he wants to go to the Anchor Academy.

We need family (the only person Alistair will relate to) to agree with us and persuade Alistair and his lawyer to do what the DA said.

This moves us to Monday evening . . . .

O Lord, how I feel so out of control! And I know that is exactly the way You want it so that we can step back and see the salvation of the Lord!

I picked up family, and we traveled home.

The conversation was very stressful. There were lots of accusations made against us as parents and people of God, in general.

Family interestingly said, "You're not gonna send him somewhere where they'll push Christianity down his throat, are you?"

I answered, "It is a school, an excellent school."

Family was lashing out at whomever they could. It was painful—but nothing like Calvary. Thank You, Lord!

Family wanted to have much dialogue with my husband and me; it was very, very tense!

Alistair has been in jail from Friday till Tuesday morning.

Chapter 6

Mission: Possible!

Matthew 10:16 tells us, "Behold, I send you forth as sheep in the midst of wolves: be ye therefore wise as serpents, and harmless as doves." Praise God for His Word!

By faith, we believed that GOD would do what only GOD can do, and that is to be excellent, and we believed that He would invite us in to be a part of it. We waited until family went to sleep and pulled out the contract that we had to sign and send to the Anchor Academy and that the DA had to review before we could send our son away. Think about it . . . we have allowed laws to be passed where the government tells us what we can and cannot do with or for our children! Oh, see how we have lost control over our children and family? I have been asleep on my watch, and I pray You would forgive me, O Lord!

Our society has become a very child-centric and feminized environment. Everything is built around the child instead of the child being integrated into the family. And if that were not enough, we've allowed a handful of people to feminize everything! A boy is a boy—not a gender-neutral being! Have mercy, Lord!

Log Entry: Tuesday Morning, September 11, 2001

God said, "Trust Me."

I told the Lord that I trusted Him.

We are at court. Today, we need to have Alistair accept the judge's/court's mandate and say he wants to go to the Academy.

When he does that, he will be adjudicated to juvenile court.

The fearful thought of the lawyer trying to do some last-minute "I can win this thing, Alistair; I can get you off as an adult, and then you can go and live with family"-type maneuvering came to mind. I don't know if the thought was from the evil one or if the Lord was showing me what to bind and loose. I did not want anything to be bungled!

Family, my husband, and I sat in an isolated room and waited for Alistair to arrive from the jail.

Detective Heap, Mr. McMerinan (the lawyer), and Mr. Bolden (the DA) spoke to us.

Now it was up to GOD, family, and Alistair.

It is always good to have family on the team.

Alistair snarls when he sees us, and the power of who is influencing him makes him livid and vile when we come near. We therefore stay our distance and pray as God orchestrates His sovereign plan to save our boy's life and give him another chance. We did not go into the courtroom; we remained in the waiting room, and family went in to see Alistair. Thank You, God!

Family said, "Hey, guy!"

He looked up and said to family, "Hey, I knew that you would come!"

Family said that they hugged and kissed him, and he lit up and smiled. (I praise God that he had family to hug.)

They told him that he needed to do what they told him to do—trust them, and do not deviate from their words.

He said that he trusted them and said that he would not deviate from their words.

They went into the court, and God spoke through family 'Alistair' lawyer! Glory to God!

Last evening, Deb and I were talking about Balaam's donkey, how it spoke to Balaam, how the prophet could only say the things that God wanted him to say, even after he received the enemy's instruction and money to curse the children of Israel.

God spoke through these vessels!

Proverbs 21:1 says, "The king's heart is in the hand of the LORD, as the rivers of water: he turneth it whithersoever he will." Glory! Glory!

Alistair allowed family to rub him; he put his hand on their shoulder, and they loved up on him.

God is so good!

My husband and I were in the waiting area while court procedures were going on, and much like Paul and Silas, we were singing hymns to the Lord in our captivity, and there was no television in the waiting room. However, there was a television in the courtroom. In the midst of our praise and worship, family rushed into the waiting area where we were and said, "They've just bombed the World Trade Center!" We could not believe it and ran out of the waiting area to see two closed-circuit TVs just outside the courtroom. We did not know who "they" were at the time, but we did know that they were our enemies.

As we continued to watch the television, we witnessed a second plane fly into the second tower. We would later discover that another plane, full of God's heroes, was able to take down their plane eighty-five miles outside of Pittsburgh, Pennsylvania. This plane was targeting the White House. The last plane hit the Pentagon, where several of my friends worked for the DOD. Have mercy, Lord! Please forgive us and have mercy!

September 11, 2001, will go down in infamy!

Because of the tragedy, Judge Ninety, Mr. Bolden, Mr. McMannan, and others expeditiously signed papers to get Alistair over to juvenile court and to start the trial. They were not sure of the state of our nation and did not want Alistair to be held up in a bureaucratic circle of paperwork and lost files. Time was of the essence. If Alistair had not arrived at the school before they went on tour, he would have to wait several months, and only God knows what nefarious activities he would be into if he stayed under the devil's influence. Yes, only God knew. God had moved on everyone's heart to get this boy to the Anchor Academy! God can and will move heaven and earth for His sovereign purposes.

Alistair was sent to the Montgomery County Youth Center under the care of Mr. Jim Costly. Family continued to love up on him, and we were so happy that he had some contact with someone who loved him. As Alistair was leaving, he asked family, "How did you get here?" They said, "I didn't walk here, did I? How do you think I got here?" He said, "My parents brought you." They said, "Yes, and your parents love you and have been working very hard on your behalf."

Alistair will go to juvenile court tomorrow and then eventually to Montana.

God is awesome!

God is perfecting those "things" that concern us!

On the heels of all this:

- We received several health care bills.
- We received taxes for the church to be filed.
- A petition has been signed against us not to be able to open our church because several neighbors said that we would be a detriment to the neighborhood.

O God, You have given us a testimony!

Time is of the essence!

We must pray for our president!

God, dear God, have mercy on America!
Bless our Commander in Chief who is at the helm.
Thousands of our countrymen and women are gone.
Hundreds of our first responders are gone.
Have mercy on us, O Lord. Have mercy!

Log Entry: Sunday, September 16, 2001

Recap from September 12 – 16, 2001:

Glory to God Most High! It truly grieves me how all the family members are acting toward my husband (especially) and me.

They are disrespecting him and being offensive. We will hold our tongues until the appointed time.

My husband, family, and I arrived at juvenile court, and it became crowded very quickly. Everyone is told to be there by 9 A.M.

We did not have to wait long before we were called in.

Prior to entering the courtroom, we met with the DA and probation officer. They were wonderful!

We requested the probation officer speak to the lawyer about the agreement that was made the day before. I felt in my spirit that the lawyer would be energized by the devil and sway Alistair to fight this in the courts as an adult. The possibility of his being with grown men, decadence, and so on literally made me ill.

The probation officer did as promised.

We went into the courtroom, and Alistair was there . . . looking intentionally unkept, like a zombie.

Alistair would not look at us, and we knew better than to look at him. He would snarl and stare at us with reddish brown slits for eyes whenever we made eye contact with him, and we did not want to provoke him into not cooperating with the court. Therefore, we held our heads down to our chests, as in submission to God, not the devil, and silently prayed.

Everything was ready to go, and Alistair was going to take the stand.

However, as the Lord had revealed to me, just as Alistair was getting out of his seat, the lawyer was energized by the devil and grabbed Alistair's arm and started whispering in his ear.

This rightly concerned us, and we continued to pray.

When the DA asked the same questions that he and the other DA had asked the previous day, instead of saying, "I want to go to school," Alistair started muttering, "It was self-defense."

Well, I almost fainted!

I started crying and saying softly, "Have mercy, Lord. Please have mercy!"

The DA tried again, and Alistair started muttering repeatedly, "It was self-defense."

I started to cry aloud. I cried out even louder, "Have mercy, Lord. Please have mercy!"

Alistair held his head down and would not make eye contact with family.

The DA, judge, and probation officer were appalled by the lawyer's behavior.

The lawyer was trying to coax Alistair to go back to adult court and beat the case there. Bottom line: As a court-appointed lawyer, he wanted Alistair 's case to go on forever so that he could be paid.

By this time, I was screaming, "Have mercy, Lord. Please have mercy!" and would not be silenced.

My husband said that I was so pitiful that our God touched the judge's heart to intercede on our behalf.

The judge interceded and said to Alistair, "Alistair, do you understand that if you don't agree to the charges, just as you did yesterday, you will go to jail?"

"Mr. DA, please explain to Alistair how much time he will have to face." The DA explained to Alistair that he would be sent back to adult prison and sentenced ten years.

After the DA's explanation, the judge turned toward Alistair and asked him what he wanted to do.

I started sobbing uncontrollably and cried out ever the more, "Have mercy, Lord. Please have mercy!"

It seemed like an eternity, but Alistair finally looked at family and then said, "The first thing you said."

The judge said, "I'll take that to mean that you want to go to school."

Alistair said, "Yeah."

Glory to God Almighty!

It was finished!

I started waving my hands and praising the Lord to the top of my lungs! God showed Himself strong on our behalf. Hallelujah!

After we all exited, my beloved tried to touch family's arm to tell family something (i.e., to let Alistair know that my husband would also have to go to court and that he did not get off easy), and family snatched away from him.

My husband was so hurt.

He had never seen family behave in such a malevolent manner.

We drove over to the visitation section, where Alistair now was, and again, he would not speak to me.

Family acted as a go-between.

My husband and I were so thankful to God for His mercy and grace!

Hallelujah! Our son was out of the penal system.

Look at God!

We were concerned that Alistair would be placed in a cell with another boy and get into an altercation. This would certainly cause the system to pull him back in. However,

God prepared a room for Alistair where there was no one but him. He ate, slept, and exercised alone.

Now was the time to pray for safe passage with no incidents. Thank You, Lord!

Chapter 7

Arrival at the Anchor

Log Entry: Thursday, September 20, 2001

Our nation is in such turmoil, yet God is still in control of every detail.

The detectives picked up Alistair on Sunday from the youth center. We were there to see him off.

I spoke to him inside of the center and told him that I loved him, and he forgot for a minute that he was not speaking to us and replied, "I love you too, Mom," and then he caught himself and shut down.

Alistair was handcuffed and escorted to the detective's van. When he got to our car, my beloved husband sat in the driver's seat. Alistair looked at his father and had a demonic/ snarling smile on his face as if to say, "Yeah, I'm out of your hands, and I have the last laugh." My husband did not smile back, but later told me that he thought to himself, *You have no idea that God/we will have the last laugh, Alistair.*

There were two retired detectives and one detective's son in the van to escort Alistair to the Anchor. They wanted to make sure that Alistair had coverage at all times and they would not be in danger. We had to sign a form that essentially stated that if Alistair accosted them or became a threat, they would attempt to subdue him. In addition, if necessary, if in a scuffle, if he were to have a fatal accident, we absolved them of any liability. That was a hard form to sign, but we believed God for Alistair's safe passage and God's redemption of his life, so we signed the form.

We did not hear from the detectives until today, Thursday, September 20, 2001, and they called to give us an update.

The detectives said that during the trip, Alistair refused to eat food. He digested an entire bag of candy and became sick on the way. The van broke down on the way and had to be repaired. In addition, approximately two hours before they arrived at the Anchor, Alistair became salty because he could not have any more candy. The detective told him that if Alistair did not stop acting in an insolent manner, the detective would put the cuffs and shackles back on him.

The detectives said something very interesting about Alistair's behavior the closer they approached the Anchor. Alistair had no idea that he was fifteen minutes or less from the Academy, but the devil knew it. They said that Alistair started acting restless, twitching, and stressing out. They thought that was strange, but did not correlate the spiritual significance of the warfare that was going on.

They said that they arrived at the Anchor and Alistair called family to let them know he was okay. He did not call us. He saw the other young men in uniform, but did not realize what was in store for him.

That evening at dinner, Alistair was restrained because he would not bow his head to say grace; he used horrible superlatives about the Word of God and said horrible things about his parents.

Glory to God! The demonic spirit is showing its true colors because its reign is just about over. It is over, in Jesus' name! Glory to God!

When Alistair did not comply, he was surprised by the peer response. He had never seen young boys dedicated/loyal to the Lord like that.

Our prayer is that God continues to soften Alistair's heart so that the Word of God can take root in good soil.

We trust You, Lord!

Alistair is healed, in Jesus' name!

I know much has happened in my son's life, and I know that we all are being transformed more and more into the image of our Lord Jesus Christ.

The Lord spoke to my spirit two weeks ago and said that He was going to do a "quick" work, and He did!

He was true to His promises!

Even down to the wire, God told me that just like Joseph, Alistair had been in the pit, the prison, and by Sunday, Alistair would be on his way to the palace (the Anchor), and he was!

The Lord is our Strong Tower!

Blessed be the name of the Lord!

Oh, if we had just known the signs!

The red flags and signs were his asking for a black painted room, stopping drinking milk (makes a man strong), being addicted to candy, lashing out at fellow students in a cowardly way after the fact, and absolute disdain for his parents and somewhat his brother.

But, if it had not been for the Lord's being on our side, where would we be?

Dearest Lord, thank You for provision!

Log Entry: Monday, September 24, 2001

Glory to the Lamb that was slain!

We cannot slack our riding!

God is raising up a generation of young people (Sons I and II) who are sold out for the Lord Jesus!

These young people will stand when they have done all to stand!

Alistair, Jesus is your Savior, son.

ALISTAIR, Jesus is your LORD.

Log Entry: Tuesday, September 25, 2001

Holy is the Lord, God Almighty!

We praise God because He is worthy to be Praised!

Today, I let my breastplate down, but God has been merciful to me, a sinner.

My husband and I had to meet with Children's Services today at 7 P.M. with Mr. Dan Miller.

However, prior to the meeting, I received in the mail a flier from a church on "Devil-Proofing Your Family."

I immediately became offended because I *felt* ("for we walk by faith, not by sight," 2 Corinthians 5:7) that people close to us had divulged our family affairs to their friends and now the leaders of a particular church were having a conference at our expense.

What an idiot I was, listening to the whispers of the devil.

My beloved husband immediately saw it as a blessing, that other families would be saved because of it.

I had to repent because I did not. I was self-centered, prideful, ashamed, and hurt. I totally responded in the flesh. Please forgive me, Lord!

We met with Mr. Dan and let him know that Alistair was a sweet and good kid, in the suburbs, who had gotten ahold of some gangsta rap. Mr. Dan assumed that a nice home and surroundings overwhelmed Alistair.

The conversation went well, and we had an opportunity to let Mr. Dan know that we lived like "this" in the inner city.

Interestingly enough, Mr. Dan explained that Alistair told the authorities the same thing. Mr. Dan recapped that the authorities were questioning Alistair and alluded that "he must have been overwhelmed by his new beautiful home, belongings, and environment." Mr. Dan said that Alistair told them that the suburbs did not impress him because he always lived in a beautiful home, had many possessions, and attended the best schools.

After Mr. Dan left, my husband ministered to me again, and then we had prayer.

I confessed my sin against God in the presence of my beloved.

God forgave me; I know it.

I accepted His forgiveness and trusted Him for the results.

I feel that the Lord spoke to my Spirit yesterday and let me know that Alistair would be back sooner than I think. We are not empty nesters, but instead, we are to utilize this time to grow, establish, and mature God's ministry. Alistair is a 2 Corinthians 5:17 man! God is making my Son II brand new! Glory to God!

I spoke to Rev. Hoyle from the Anchor today; Alistair was having his educational diagnostic test accomplished today.

Alistair spoke to Pastor Hoyle today; he had not previously spoken. God is turning Alistair's heart toward Him. Thank You, Lord!

We receive the promises of God through faith in the Lord Christ Jesus. Amen!

Log Entry: Thursday, September 27, 2001

To God be the glory for the thing He hath done!
I miss my son so much!
Every day I look at his pictures and just want to lose it!
But God causes me to rejoice because my son's mind and all of him is being renewed! Glory! Hallelujah!

Alistair is a new creation in Christ Jesus! Old things are passed away! Behold, all things are become new! Thank You, Lord, for Alistair's new life! Bless You, Lord!

Log Entry: Friday, October 5, 2001

On Friday, we received a call from Brother Dennis and Pastor Hoyle from the Anchor. We also received a letter from our precious Alistair. I was upset with the letter and its contents until my husband ministered to me. Alistair referred to us using my husband's name and my name in the letter. He said that he would have rather gone to jail if he had known that we were sending him to this place. He said that this place was the worst possible place that we could have sent him to.

That was confirmation for us that the Anchor Academy for Boys was, therefore, a great place and the right place for our boy! Hallelujah!

Alistair went on to say we should have sent him to military school.

One of the many horrific things that has happened during Alistair's displacement/disconnect between him and us is that the "system" told him that he had rights. He feels/felt that he had a certain amount of *power* removed from us.

I praise God for keeping Alistair in His loving care.

Another short-lived manifestation of the demonic influence on Alistair is the spirit of prejudice.

Alistair would not touch the doorknobs that white students touched.

It all disgusted us so; to think that our son was acting like an imbecile was a real blow.

However, these men are not playing with Alistair. They made him backtrack all of his steps and reopen every door that he would not touch.

I felt so bad, but Pastor Hoyle and Brother Dennis said, "But that's what we are here for!"

God is so merciful!

Alistair and the other students are going on tour for three weeks in October 2001.

I spoke with Pastor Hoyle, and we believe God for the manifestation of Alistair's salvation.

We know that it is done, in Jesus' name.

The Lord was reminding me of how His mercies are new every day. The Lord was reminding me of how Alistair will return a man of integrity! The Lord was reminding me that my Alistair, the Alistair who refused to die until he could behold the Christ with his own eyes, would emerge some day. Glory to God!

My Alistair is a man of integrity.

Prayer: Please save the Gangsta rappers that Alistair has been listening to and help Alistair never to return to his own vomit like a dog.

Log Entry: Sunday, October 7, 2001

My husband was ordained a reverend today. The enemy was trying to destroy God's ministry before it was even started. God has been so merciful to us!

Log Entry: Friday, October 12, 2001

We received a letter from Alistair that should have never gotten through, in my opinion. It was so "raw." It was vulgar, and he called us every curse word in the book! I was so shocked! I did not know my *"baby boy"* even knew such words. What an eye-opening experience!

Our godchildren came over to play G.I. Joe with my husband; that delighted him, and he was blessed!

We went to see our eldest son play football, and he made a lot of tackles. He was also inducted into his little league football team's (the Panthers) Hall of Fame.

Thank You, Lord, for giving us some rest and recreation.

Log Entry: Wednesday, October 17, 2001

Yesterday marked a month that Alistair went on his way to the Anchor Academy for Boys. I was feeling oppressed and sad.

A dear sister in the Lord sent me an email and wrote the following:

> Alistair's heart was like an unkept garden.
>
> It was once kept, but now it is unkept.
>
> God is listening to the prayers of the saints, and God is breaking up the fallow ground.
>
> Just like a thief, the devil came in to steal, kill, and destroy the ministry.
>
> He couldn't get your husband, Son I, or you, so he went after the apple of everyone's eye, which was Alistair. Alistair was the weak link.
>
> God is breaking up the ground, mixing up the dirt, picking out the weeds, and taking out the rocks.
>
> God has sown good seed on newly irrigated soil.
>
> Don't be moved by the facts (Alistair's letters and things).
>
> Believe God for the manifestation of the grass.
>
> There are rich, green, colored blades.

Glory to God!

Later in the day, I called Pastor Hoyle to see:

- If Alistair was okay.
- Where in Modesto, California, we should call to speak with him.
- If they cashed our check.

Pastor Hoyle said that as far as he knew, Alistair was fine.

I told him about the rap lyrics pertaining to suicide in Alistair's letters and all the profane statements throughout his letters to his father and me.

Pastor Hoyle said that the usual person who reads letters probably did not read that letter because it should not have gone out; they would make him rewrite it.

We told him that we responded by writing a letter with a love song to Alistair. Pastor Hoyle laughed.

(This was our mistake. You do not make deals with the devil, and you do not coddle him. It was actually good that we saw the letter; it allowed us to see the depravity of his mind and gave enlightenment on how to pray for our son.)

Then, look at God!

Pastor Hoyle started talking about God breaking up fallow ground in Alistair's heart. Nevertheless, good seed is falling on the irrigated soil.

Glory to God! "At the mouth of two witnesses, or at the mouth of three witnesses, shall the matter be established" (Deuteronomy 19:15b). Hallelujah! Thank You for Your confirmation, O Lord!

Pastor Hoyle said that the staff thinks Alistair is handsome and reminds them of Deion Sanders if they could imagine Alistair smiling. I laughed because Alistair always loved Deion Sanders. Pastor Hoyle said that it would be great if Deion Sanders and Reggie White could spend the day at the Anchor.

Pastor Hoyle also said that (he was not sure if it was a dream or a vision) he saw Alistair crying out to the Lord during the singing of a particular song that the young men sing when they are out ministering.

Then he said that he had this dream or vision about Alistair at about 3:33 in the morning.

I quietly told him that my boy was born at 3:33 on a Sunday morning.

79

I receive that as a confirmation of a new birth/life for our son.

Praises be to our God!

Log Entry: Sunday, October 21, 2001

I love You, I love You,
I love You, Lord, today,
Because You cared for me in such a precious way!
And Lord, I love You, I lift You up, and I magnify Your
name! That's why my heart is filled with praise!

Glory! Glory!

Today we met in our newest sanctuary (our basement), and my beloved has done a wonderful job! Since the township voted not to allow us to open a church because it would be detrimental to the neighborhood, we decided to refurbish our basement and use it for the Lord's work that He has given us to do.

Alistair will come home to an established ministry. I often look at his picture that my sister had taken long ago with all four boys, and my Alistair is so beautiful. Lord, I miss my son so much!

The Lord is so faithful!

The Lord told me to believe Him and not waver!

Saints of God, we have to depend on God for everything—our deliverance, our children's deliverance, and so on.

God is faithful, and He will do it!

We get to call Alistair this week! Thank You, Lord! We believe God! Amen!

Log Entry: Tuesday, October 23, 2001

I am reminded of the song "Because He Lives," which lets me know I can face tomorrow without fear!

Glory to God!

This morning, I called Brother Dennis and spoke to him about our much-anticipated telephone call to our Alistair this evening.

I asked if he saw any blades of grass come up out of the ground of Alistair's heart, and he told me he has seen some blades shooting forward out of Alistair's heart.

(He said that Alistair is manipulative, skillful in influencing or controlling others to his own advantage.)

He said that Alistair laughs and enjoys watching the other children participate in and have fun playing games. However, he stops laughing if he sees Brother Dennis watching him.

(He said that Alistair is spiteful, showing malicious ill will and a desire to hurt.)

Log Entry: Evening of Tuesday, October 23, 2001

We told Brother Dennis that Alistair always stood on the Word of God, even if no one else did. Brother Dennis said that he allowed Alistair's nasty letter to get through because he wanted us to see Alistair's true heart condition. The second nasty letter did not make it through because it contained the words to an entire song by a rapper. In addition to the song, at the bottom of this particular letter, Alistair wrote that he sold his soul to the devil when he was living with us.

Look at God's mercy and grace!

Thank You, Lord, for not allowing the devil to wipe us out!

Brother Dennis said that Alistair wants to do anything that would hurt his parents.

We coordinated to call Alistair at Liberty Baptist Church this evening.

We attempted to reach Alistair several times, but the Anchor boys had not yet arrived in Modesto, California. Finally, we were able to connect.

Brother Dennis told Alistair that his dad was on the telephone, and Alistair said that he did not want to speak to us. Brother Dennis said, "Okay, you can leave." After Alistair left the room, Brother Dennis told us again that Alistair was manipulative and spiteful.

Brother Dennis said that we would have to back off for a while and not write or call Alistair. But we are to keep in touch with Brother Dennis, and he will let us know how Alistair is doing.

Brother Dennis said that eventually, Alistair would ask him, "Why haven't I heard from my parents?" That is when Brother Dennis will remind Alistair that he chose not to communicate with us. Alistair, theoretically, will request to speak with us. Then Brother Dennis will say, "Okay, Alistair; now we will do it the right way."

Glory to God!

Log Entry: Wednesday, October 24, 2001

Today I spoke with Donna, and we shared about rebellion. She said that God was not a "waster." She said (and we all agree) that running after his affections would only cause Alistair to rise up against us even more.

My God is so awesome!

Isaiah 59:19 says, "So shall they fear the name of the LORD from the west, and his glory from the rising of the sun. When the enemy shall come in like a flood, the Spirit of the LORD shall lift up a standard against him." Thank You, Lord Jesus!

My prayer: "Be careful for nothing; but in every thing by prayer and supplication with thanksgiving let your requests be made known unto God. And the peace of God, which passeth all understanding, shall keep your hearts and minds through Christ Jesus" (Philippians 4:6-7).

Log Entry: Saturday, November 3, 2001

We praise GOD for HIS faithfulness!

During the past week, I spoke with Delores, who is a lovely woman of God who works at the Anchor Academy for Boys. Delores is the cook and broke several ribs a while back and is now working in the office.

She said that she saw Alistair smile. She said that he tries to cover his face when he does; nevertheless, he smiles.

We praise God!

Glory to God! God is breaking up the fallow ground. We thank God and praise Him for all that He hath done, is doing, and will continue to do! Glory to the Lamb!

Today we received letter number 5 from Alistair. It was written with the best handwriting that we've seen in years (even prior to this situation).

In his letter, he talked about wanting to live with family and said that he missed his cousin.

In his letter, he gave lots of information to tell his cousin regarding what he should and should not do. He said that other relatives and their siblings were good people and inferred that his nuclear family was not. At the end of the letter, Alistair fabricated a "let me get you back/demonic scripture." The "scripture" was very grisly, and it was to the effect that "thou shalt not attempt to take a soul that has already been given to another." It baffled us, and we did not really understand the depths of our situation.

We started shouting with praise unto God and countered with, "God will redeem the young man of God! And God will redeem the time!

Hebrews 11:6 reminds me, "But without faith it is impossible to please him: for he that cometh to God must believe that he is, and that he is a rewarder of them that diligently seek him." God is able! God is God! Glory to God! There is nothing too hard for God!

Log Entry: Tuesday, November 6, 2001

Majesty! Worship His majesty! Unto Jesus Christ, our Savior and Lord!

Hearsay! How disheartening! Today we heard of Alistair's ordeal via my very dear friend. She ran into an acquaintance, and he spewed forth numerous derogatory statements about my husband and me. His information was skewed, but just like the devil, it had enough event doctrine to determine who his source was and from where the erroneous hearsay generated. We cannot shut the mouths of the naysayer, but God can. She said she defended our parenting skills and that I was not a horrible daughter and family member. We thank God for His mercy and grace—and how He will get the glory out of this situation.

Thank You, Jesus!

Log Entry: Wednesday, November 7, 2001

When I think about what God hath done for me, I will open up my heart to everyone I see and say, "Jesus Christ is the way!"

The Lord is holy and has proved Himself to His people.

God loves us and offers redemption for all who will receive the Lord Jesus as Savior. Thank You, Lord!

Today I shared with family how I felt betrayed by them, bearing my nuclear family's life to the world. They became insulted that I was upset. That's the way of the world; we see it every day! Jesus told us that right will be called wrong and wrong will be called right. God will sustain us! God will sustain us! God will sustain us! God's mercy and grace and the blood of Jesus sooth our wounded souls and emotions. Glory to God Almighty!

Log Entry: Thursday, November 8, 2001

God told me to praise Him for the victory right now! I did! God said there is proof in the pudding! God is bringing him out!

Therefore if any man be in Christ, he is a new creature: old things are passed away; behold, all things are become new.

2 Corinthians 5:17

Glory to God!

Log Entry: Saturday, November 10, 2001

But ye, beloved, building up yourselves on your most holy faith, praying in the Holy Ghost.

Jude 20

Lord, please forgive me because I have not been doing the work that You have given to my hands to do.
I felt the Lord minister this to me:

"Depend on Me. You cannot pull it off by yourself. It will take more, but I have given you the time. Redeem the time, for your son will return.

"Your son is sad today. I have softened his heart. I am making memories for him. He will never want to be separated from his family again. Glory to God!

"Resume praying in Alistair's room. We have taken back the territory. We have occupied it with our troops. Fill his room with prayer and power. He is no longer a dormant young man, and thus his room will no longer be dormant. Remember, daughter? Remember? We cleaned this room with the Word of God! What was once foul and barren is now full of light. The work is done. Occupy, occupy, occupy, occupy until I return. Amen!"

See? You will see the manifestation!

Log Entry: Monday, November 12, 2001

My dear sister in the Lord and I have been fasting and praying for a while. Some of the things we have been praying about are our children, salvation for family members, and finances. During prayer today, the Holy Spirit spoke to me and said that He is in Alistair, and He is rising up in Alistair. And soon, He will reign in his mortal body. I believe the Lord spoke, "The Spirit of the Lord GOD is upon [my sons]; because the LORD hath anointed [them] to preach good tidings unto the meek; he hath sent [them] to bind up the brokenhearted, to proclaim liberty to the captives, and the opening of the prison to them that are bound" (Isaiah 61:1).

God: "Tell Me I can have My way with Alistair."
Me: "God, You can have Your way with Alistair."
God: "I have him in the palm of My hands."
Glory to God!

Then said the LORD unto me, Thou hast well seen: for I will hasten my word to perform it.

Jeremiah 1:12

And he shall turn the heart of the fathers to the children, and the heart of the children to their fathers, lest I come and smite the earth with a curse.

Malachi 4:6

Log Entry: Tuesday, November 13, 2001

My beloved husband spoke to Brother Dennis this evening about Alistair. Brother Dennis said that Alistair is doing well in school. He is doing very well in working (manual labor) at the academy. He is laughing at the appropriate times, he sings songs, he recites Scriptures, and he is being sociable with the other boys.

Brother Dennis is encouraged, but said that Alistair is still not showing any remorse for his actions.

Glory to God! God is willing to forgive abundantly!

God wants to abundantly pardon!

Alistair still writes not-so-great correspondence to his dad and me. We are still referred to by our first names.

Alistair wants to know why other family members have not written to him.

Caution to parents: It is important for our children to connect with God and then their parents. This is the godly and natural order of things. This is one of the major tenets of the ministry. We realize it is necessary not to thwart the success of the ministry by being visceral and yielding to our own desires for our son's happiness. Happiness means what is happening now. God wants us to have His joy! We thank God for His Word.

Romans 1:28-32 says:

[28]And even as they did not like to retain God in their knowledge, God gave them over to a reprobate mind, to do those things which are not convenient; [29]being filled with all unrighteousness, fornication, wickedness, covetousness, maliciousness; full of envy, murder, debate, deceit, malignity; whisperers, [30]backbiters, haters of God, despiteful, proud, boasters, inventors of evil things, disobedient to

parents, [31]without understanding, covenantbreakers, without natural affection, implacable, unmerciful: [32]who knowing the judgment of God, that they which commit such things are worthy of death, not only do the same, but have pleasure in them that do them.

When any of us are in a state of rebellion against God, all of the above and more are present.

We do not retain God in our knowledge. We do not acknowledge Him and His Word. God is long-suffering with us, but will eventually hand us over to a reprobate (abandoned/condemned way of thinking) mind to do things that are sinful—for example, "being filled with all unrighteousness, fornication, wickedness, covetousness, maliciousness; full of envy, murder, debate, deceit, malignity; whisperers, backbiters, haters of God, despiteful, proud, boasters, inventors of evil things, **disobedient to parents.**"

Parents are God's representatives here on earth. Godly parents are the *Holy Spirit* to a child in that *they* lead and guide that child into all truth.

Rebellious people are without understanding; covenant-breakers are without **natural affection.** They are implacable and unmerciful. We sometimes mistakenly think "without **natural affection**" has to do with sexual orientation, and so on. That is not the case. God used Brother Dennis to break down the Scriptures so that parents could clearly see how it pertains to our boys. In the above Scriptures, the apostle Paul initially talked about God's making a case for Himself with mankind. Mankind ignored God and was wise in their own conceit and became fools (see vv. 19-22). Paul then speaks about the idols they made. When we are in rebellion, we sit on the throne of our hearts; Jesus does not have that position. We see this in verse 23. Then Paul covers unclean/lustful and improper use of the body in verses 24-27. Therefore, the "without **natural affection**" means exactly that. Children are supposed to *naturally* love their parents; parents are supposed to *naturally* love their children. However, when we are in rebellion, we lose **natural affection**, mercy, and so on. We do vile things.

Thank You, Lord!

Log Entry: Monday, December 10, 2001

Yes, Lord, completely yes! My soul says yes!

The Lord is good! A Strong Tower! He covers and comforts His own!

Family members accompanied me to a Christian play, "Miracle of Christmas."

On the way, I asked them not to reveal private conversations to anyone because I had become painfully aware that people were talking about our situation with people who normally would not have any knowledge of our family affairs.

They really did not comprehend my train of thought, and I guess rightly so. We spoke two different languages . . . carnal vs. spiritual. I had to repent for even expressing myself. Two prophets told me not to be responsive to people talking, but I was hurt, and I was going to speak my peace, again. O Lord, please forgive me! What a bratty thing I did!

I prayed and asked my Father to forgive me and to take back any territory that I had given the enemy of my soul. Isn't it good to have a good God?

God is so faithful!

We have received more letters from our precious Alistair, and they have been negative. Alistair often speaks of how he is tired of living.

Alistair told Brother Dennis that he was raised well.

He said that he did not deserve to be raised well.

He said that he did not want to live with us anymore.

Brother Dennis was perplexed and weary when he spoke with my husband. Brother Dennis cannot understand why

Alistair's heart has not been broken yet. It is hard for all of us to discern why he does not want contact with us, his parents.

Brother Dennis said that Alistair is very compliant, but still execrable in the rebellion arena.

I think Alistair really does not understand we are all under authority to someone. However, Brother Dennis does not want Alistair to use this "detachment" arena to his personal advantage, either.

God loves us so very much! We bless the Lord forevermore!

We were allowed to do something special for Alistair for Christmas. Thank You, Lord!

God has already worked it out! Hallelujah, and thank You, Lord!

Log Entry: Friday, December 14, 2001

We went to court today, and we had a fine lawyer represent us. It cost us $500. Our lawyer wanted to fight the case, but we instructed him to allow the court to fine us $300, and we gladly paid it. Daddy's part is over. Now, we believe for complete acquittal for our Alistair.

> And they departed from the presence of the council, rejoicing that they were counted worthy to suffer shame for his name.
>
> Acts 5:41

What a privilege to suffer shame for Christ's sake! Glory to God!

Log Entry: Sunday, December 23, 2001

We have an awesome God!

Earlier this week, we sent Christmas presents to our Alistair. We love and miss him sooooo much!

On Friday, I spoke to Brother Dennis about my "baby boy." Brother Dennis said that Alistair was compliant and does everything that he is told to do, but he is very angry with God. He is also slacking with his schoolwork. Glory; we believe God!

One thing is for certain: God is faithful! Hallelujah!

Today during church service, my beloved was preaching on redemption. Glory to God!

I was not necessarily thinking about my baby boy at the moment; however, the Holy Spirit witnessed inside of my spirit that He was redeeming Alistair. Glory to God!

God has done the work, in Jesus' name!

Log Entry: Monday, December 24, 2001

When we called on Friday, December 21, 2001, Brother Dennis told us that we could call Alistair on Monday at 11:00 our time.

We called, and Alistair spoke to us! Oh, how we smiled!

It was "estranged," but it was the first time since August (four months) that he had spoken to us!

God loves us so much!

Before Alistair came to the telephone, Brother Dennis told us that Alistair almost broke in chapel the other night, and that he has seen a change in Alistair's demeanor in the last few days.

Look at God!

We declare, "Alistair's mind is the mind of Christ, in Jesus' name!"

I declare that Alistair will never be estranged from his family again, in Jesus' name!

Log Entry: Tuesday, December 25, 2001

CHRISTMAS DAY! GLORY TO GOD!
PEACE ON EARTH AND GOOD WILL TOWARD MEN.

Christmas was not the same without our youngest son. We have a tradition on Christmas morning. Alistair's daddy gives me the twelve days of Christmas gifts. Eleven of the gifts are usually horrific or very nominal, and then he gives me something precious. The boys always laughed themselves to tears as they watched the various expressions on my face as I opened each gift and struggled to find something nice to say about it.

We are thankful that Christ died for our sins and that God graciously spared our lives. Merry Christmas and happy birthday, Lord Jesus!

Log Entry: Tuesday January 1, 2002

But seek ye first the kingdom of God, and his righteousness; and all these things shall be added unto you.

Matthew 6:33

Jesus! Jesus! You are the Living Word!

We give God glory today, for He is God! So majestic is our God!

I spoke to Brother Dennis yesterday. He said that my Alistair was very compliant and doesn't want anything to do with God, his daddy, Son I, and me.

Brother Dennis said that Alistair is smiling more and interacting more with the other boys and staff, and is not quite the robot that he was.

Brother Dennis said that the chapel person said he could see Alistair being dealt with by God twice, but Alistair didn't break yet.

Brother Dennis said that they are very encouraged because although there hasn't been a 180-degree change, there is some gradual change. Moreover, whatever change happens with Alistair, it will be real.

Included in Alistair's Christmas things was a picture album telling his life from the beginning until approximately one year ago.

Brother Dennis said that Alistair looked at it in a cursory way and handed it back to him to send home. Brother Dennis kept the book.

We pray that after God breaks Alistair's heart, he will want the keepsake.

God is so awesome!

God has brought Alistair out, in Jesus' name! Glory! Glory!

Prayer: Dear God, please continue to do a new work in Alistair's heart, mind, intelligence, will, hearing, speaking, and inward and outward behavior. Our mantra is, "Therefore if any man be in Christ, he is a new creature: old things are passed away; behold, all things are become new" (2 Corinthians 5:17).

Only God can!

Only God will!

Thank You, Lord!

(Motivation of the message of reconciliation)

Therefore if any man be in Christ, he is a new creature: old things are passed away; behold, all things are become new.

2 Corinthians 5:17

The term new/mature refers to the spiritual transformation that occurs with the inner man when a person believes in Christ as Savior. The Christian is now a new man as opposed to the old man that he was before he became a Christian,

God: "Daughter, remember, 'The effectual fervent prayer of a righteous man availeth much'" (James 5:16b). Amen.

Theoretically, by the normal timetable, we are supposed to visit Alistair in January 2002; however, Brother Dennis advised us that now is not the appointed time. He would not want us to come to the Anchor and be treated badly by Alistair. How thoughtful of him.

We will follow his lead. Therefore, for now, we can call on Monday.

There is some pain in ministry right now. The Lord is showing us His mercy. The unfathomable pain and anguish we are experiencing via Alistair is preparing us for ministry. Hallelujah! Alistair is preparing us to love when rejected by men/sheep that belong to the Lord Jesus.

Thank You, Lord!

Log Entry: Wednesday, January 23, 2002

Glory to God in the highest!

In the sanctuary, in the evening, as I prayed, the Lord said that I had to say the following aloud to Him:

"Father God. Like Hannah, Samuel's mother, if you will save and deliver my son, I will dedicate him to God's service, just as she did with Samuel. And Lord, I do still want to mother him, though. In addition, God, I pray that he will not be like Samuel and allow his sons to do any old thing. My beloved did not allow our son to do just any old thing. My husband was a Titus man. He was the man of one wife with children that were not unruly. I went on and on . . . .

Then the Lord said for me to repeat the following after the unction of the Holy Spirit: "Lord, have Your perfect way in the life of my son, Alistair. Lord, have Your perfect way in the life of my son, Son I. Lord, have Your perfect way in the life of my husband. And Lord, especially in my life, I pray, have Your perfect way."

My God is an awesome wonder!

There are many confirmations that God is giving me.

There's joy at the end of the suffering!

Log Entry: Thursday, January 31, 2002

The song "Awesome God" is coming to mind.

God said: "He (Alistair) will be a great orator one day, and he will preach My Word!"

Prayer: This is an awesome book of deliverance. My beloved and I went to California on temporary duty for my job. We experienced a bomb scare in San Francisco. God is so wonderful; He made up the lost airtime. God will redeem the years that the cancer worm destroyed in Alistair's life and our family members' lives.

God: "I have given Alistair an awesome anointing for laying on of hands for healing and deliverance. I have given him a smile that will light the world." Amen.

My Lord Jesus was focused. He never stopped loving people even while they persecuted Him. Jesus is God and always remained holy in every situation.

Trust in the LORD with all thine heart; and lean not unto thine own understanding. In all thy ways acknowledge him, and he shall direct thy paths.
Proverbs 3:5-6

We had prayer today for: persecuted Christians in Somalia, all African nations, India, China, Russia, and more; missionaries near and far; our Commander in Chief; Mrs. Laura Bush; the Cabinet; and the Joint Chiefs of Staff.

Recap: Before any of the above was written today, I read from the beginning of Alistair's logbook to this date. God wanted me to stand back and see the salvation of the Lord and to firm up those assignments that I have not accomplished concerning Alistair and the ministry. In addition, there are supernatural deposited Scriptures, praying the answers, and ministry administration.

God can redeem us from the lowest depths. Thank You, Lord!

This then is the message which we have heard of him, and declare unto you, that God is light, and in Him is no darkness at all.

1 John 1:5

If we confess our sins, he is faithful and just to forgive us our sins, and to cleanse us from all unrighteousness.

1 John 1:9

I beseech you therefore, brethren, by the mercies of God, that ye present your bodies a living sacrifice, holy, acceptable unto God, which is your reasonable service. And be not conformed to this world: but be ye transformed by the renewing of your mind, that ye may prove what is that good, and acceptable, and perfect, will of God.

Romans 12:1-2

Log Entry: Saturday, February 2, 2002

Our God is an awesome wonder!

In the multitude of my thoughts [anxieties] within me thy comforts delight my soul.

Psalm 94:19

When we give all our cares to God, our worries will depart; He gives to us a peace of mind that claims our anxious heart. The more you think about God's goodness, the less you'll think about your worries.

Log Entry: Wednesday, February 13, 2002

My baby wept in chapel on Thursday, February 7, 2002. My son's countenance is changing.

God said: "Alistair will serve Me. He will be an asset to the Anchor Academy. Alistair is a powerful, loving preacher, full of God's compassion and mercy. Rejoice! Again, I say rejoice! Alistair's redemption is nigh. What a beautiful heart I have given him, one full of the love of Christ and richly saturated with the blood of the Lamb."

Hallelujah, Lord!

I prayed for teens.

I prayed for gang rappers.

God said: "The title of the memoir will be *I Took It Personally*." Amen.

Log Entry: Sunday, February 17, 2002

"I can do all things through Christ which strengtheneth me" (Philippians 4:13).

God uses weakness to reveal His great sufficiency. Therefore, if we let Him work through us, we will see His great power. To experience God's strength, we must first admit our weakness. Lord, I praise You and thank You for Alistair's salvation and deliverance today! Glory to God!

Log Entry: Monday, February 18, 2002

Glory be to the Lamb of God that was slain! I spoke with Brother Dennis today, and he said that Alistair's eyes are softening and Alistair gives better answers to questions. I told Brother Dennis that I wrote Alistair a letter and told him not to call us by our first names again. I told Alistair that we are his parents, not his peers. Then I asked if we could send birthday gifts, and he said we could, and have a three-minute conversation with him. Alistair has still not accepted Christ and does not communicate with us verbally. Nevertheless, the Lord has urged us, by the power of the Holy Spirit, to make plans to visit him. By faith, we will be obedient and go.

Our visit with Alistair will be five days and four nights and will commence on a Friday at 8 A.M.

I was listening to Raul Ries today about the end-times and was reminded how when Alistair was younger, we were doing math homework and drawing a number line. He looked up at me and exclaimed, "Mommy, how can people not believe in Jesus? We even measure time by His birth and His death." Glory to God! The Holy Spirit impressed upon me to let Brother Dennis know what Alistair had said when he was younger, and perhaps he could remind Alistair about it.

After I asked Brother Dennis the usual stuff, I told him that I wanted to share the aforementioned information with him.

I did, and he exclaimed, "That's interesting. I was just challenging a boy about the very same thing last Wednesday, and Alistair was there. That must have jolted his memory. I will remind him."

I said, "Thank you."

Afterward, I was so full of joy! God allowed Brother Dennis to encourage us! God is good! Amen.

Log Entry: Saturday, February 23, 2002

The truth from the Bible about unanswered prayer:

And it shall come to pass, that before they call, I will answer; and while they are yet speaking, I will hear.

Isaiah 65:24

Log Entry: Tuesday, February 26, 2002

Probation follow-up: Mr. Ben Jones from probation called about Alistair. He also called the Anchor Academy directly. Brother Dennis told him that initially, Alistair resisted the program, but in the last two weeks, Brother Dennis has really seen a change.

We know that God is up to something good! Lord God, please continue to break up the fallow ground. Thank You for saving Alistair and delivering him from the bondage of devil worship, witchcraft, and every other sinful behavior that is not like You. In Jesus' name, we pray with thanksgiving. Amen.

Log Entry: Monday, March 11, 2002

The Lord God is so good! Glory be to our God on high!

It is Monday morning, and although it's a scheduled Alternate Work Schedule day, I decided to go in. Then I realized that would be wasted time. Therefore, I will wait for the document to arrive, and if it makes sense, then I will go in.

Nevertheless, I wanted (i.e., the Holy Spirit encouraged me) to come aside and be with God instead of calling in and jumping back in bed.

Last Monday, we spoke to our son, and we were so blessed that God spared his life. The Lord God is good. I wrote Alistair and told him of the genesis of his name. I told him about "Alistair" the Cyrenian, Alistair the just and devout man, Alistair of the tribe of Judah, and I told him of Solomon, who asked for wisdom and understanding. I was asking God to give him an ability to "hear." "Alistair" means to hear!

I also told him a story about roaches and Raid. Roaches run when the light and Raid go into a room. The light of Christ dispels darkness. We gave him Scripture to challenge him to "come up!" Glory be to God! God has saved Alistair, by faith, in Jesus' name!

Log Entry: Thursday, April 11, 2002

The Lord is an awesome wonder! Just before I ascended the steps, I saw *that* night and remembered the cursing letters and the anguish! I cried out to the Lord because I have been responding to my feelings. I have been thin-skinned, and I have reviled when I am reviled by people the devil energizes and uses against my husband and me. Their comments and accusations are painful. Please forgive me, and I choose to forgive them, O Lord.

Flashbacks: I have been so very disgusted with myself because of my lack of Christian maturity, and I finally remembered to run to the "Rock of my salvation"! Petty, mean, evil-speaking, tantrums, and so on! It vexes me so! Have mercy, dear Lord, and help me!

I yielded to the enemy, and sour/spoiled fruit came forth, so much so that the "Ain't" that I was having ill (and I mean "old" stuff) feelings against because of the Alistair situation ministered to me!

God spoke a word: The Holy Spirit beckoned me aside and agreed with every truthful thing that I confessed about myself. Then He told me the following:

1. The attacks (same old nonsense) are because of the book! (I have started *I Took It Personally!* and it will be an awesome blessing to many.)
2. The devil is coming for the "Word" and my testimony.

3. While at our older son's college last week, as we were in praise and worship at Victory, the minister was asking, "What do you want from God?" I answered, "I wanted salvation and deliverance for my son!" The Lord showed me a vision of Alistair's heart before I started to praise Him. It was cracked down the middle.

4. After crying out to the Lord and praising Him, God told me about and then showed me a heart that had been smashed into millions of tiny pieces that could not be put back together again. Therefore, God had to give my boy a brand new heart! Glory to God!

5. God is bringing all of it to pass in His perfect timing. We just have to wait on the Lord. However, we have to occupy (in faith and virtue) until Jesus returns. No more falling for the "okeydokey!" I must tighten up my breastplate and secure my helmet and all other parts of my armor. I cannot allow myself to be "moved" or "beguiled"!

God said: "Either you believe ME, or you don't! I will do that which I promised! If it is not MY Word, cast it down. I have sheltered you, hidden you, and redeemed the time for you!" Amen.

P.S. Alistair's letters are written in much better handwriting.
P.P.S. The Lord said that He had refreshed me and to go forth in Jesus' name!

Log Entry: Monday, April 15, 2002

We called the Anchor in the morning and spoke with Brother Dennis, and he said that Alistair is the water provider and feeder for Ms. Zoie, the dog.

Zoie gets excited when she sees Alistair, but Zoie gets excited about anything.

We pray that Alistair responds to the love and attention that Zoie needs and wants to give him.

Later in the evening, we called, and Alistair answered the telephone.

My husband said, "Hello, Alistair!" and Alistair said, "Hello, Dad." Then Alistair's daddy said, "Alistair, Mommy's on the phone." Then I said, "Hello, Alistair!" and Alistair said, "Hello, Mom."

Our hearts were overjoyed! Hallelujah! God is mighty! God is awesome! God is giving him a new heart! Hallelujah!

The conversation went okay.

But look at God! We cannot minimize the great thing He hath done! We are fully convinced, we will not lose our profession!

God is restoring our fellowship with Alistair. Thank You, Lord!

On Saturday, God had me speak on "Even Now, Lord" at our Women's Fellowship. The referenced text was John 11:1-44, when Lazarus died and was raised by Christ.

Jesus can resurrect any dead thing!

God can change a situation even after the fact! In 2 Kings 4:1-37, the Shulamite woman wouldn't even acknowledge that the son God gave her, whom she never asked for, whom she loved, was dead. When asked where she was going, she answered, "It shall be well." By the time she reached the prophet and bowed down prostrate before him, she declared, "It is well." I receive that same word and declare, "It is well, in Jesus' name!"

She knew that God could do something!

Martha knew that God would still do it if Jesus asked!

God is sovereign! God heals, restores, raises the dead, and creates miracles if He chooses to.

I was listening to a man who was healed while teaching a Sunday school class. He had been a preacher and had lost his voice. He suffered much.

He was relegated to only speaking for a moment at a time now. And every once in a while, they would allow him to teach a Sunday school class. He was teaching a Sunday school class and was saying, "Sometimes we are in a pit situation (but we're not to lose heart because . . .)." As he said the word "pit," God instantaneously healed him.

The Anchor young men are going on a tour soon and will be returning just when we arrive for our visit with Alistair.

God is working in all of our lives for our good and His glory!

Only God can do it!

Only God will!

By faith, my God, my loving and gracious Lord, has already done it!

Hallelujah to the Lamb! Holy and righteous is the Lamb! Amen.

Chapter 8

The Long-Awaited News!

Log Entry: Monday, April 22, 2002

Christ is risen!
Jesus resurrects dead things! Glory to God!

Jesus Christ is the same yesterday, today, and forever!

Yesterday was Mom's birthday, and it is such a blessing to have a mom who is living and healthy. Thank You, Lord!

As I sat and pondered, I remembered how family was used in the plot to destroy Alistair. How unaware, or non-admitting, family and friends rose up against us in judgment . . . . I lamented for a while and then came under conviction of the Holy Spirit.

How many times did I miss the mark?

Please forgive me, and please have mercy on all of us, Lord!

It's all about God's grace!

Glory to God!

God will work it out!

Only God can!

Look at God!

This morning at 11:00, I called the Anchor Academy as always, and Brother Dennis answered the telephone.

Precious Sister Delores usually answers the telephone, so this was an unexpected surprise.

He said, "Hold on, because I have something to tell you that you will want to hear!"

I held on the phone and sang songs of praise to my God. It seemed like an eternity, but it was only a few minutes. Finally, Brother Dennis came back to the telephone and said, "Hold on a little longer."

I said, "No, I'm on a cell phone, and I'll call you back on a regular phone in two minutes."

However, ol' "got to utilize every second of the day" me hung up some clothes and then went upstairs to call back Brother Dennis, so it was actually longer than two minutes before I called again.

I called again, but had to hold on because Brother Dennis was still talking to someone else.

I was poised to stay still and do nothing except wait to hear from Brother Dennis. After a while, Brother Dennis came back to the phone and said, "Well, at about 2:00 or 3:00 this morning, your Alistair got saved!"

I let out a shout and, "Hallelujah!" and, "Thank You, Jesus!" and, "Glory to God!" and so on.

I cried and carried on and said, "Oops! I'm sorry!" Then I said, "No, no, I'm not sorry!"

Then I began to weep and shout again!

Glory to God!

Then I asked Brother Dennis just what happened.

Brother Dennis said that at around 2:00 or 3:00 this morning, Alistair went to Brother Caleb and said, "Excuse me, sir."

Brother Caleb thought that Alistair wanted to go to the bathroom because they have to ask permission to go to the bathroom in the middle of the night.

So Caleb said, "Yes, Alistair, you may go to the bathroom."

Alistair said, "No sir, I don't need to go to the bathroom; I need to be saved."

So right there, next to Brother Caleb's bed, Alistair knelt down, Brother Caleb led Alistair in the sinner's prayer, and Alistair accepted the Lord Jesus into his heart.

I cried, and I shouted!

I made Brother Dennis repeat it for me again.

Brother Dennis said that there was a boy in a nearby bunk who heard everything, and now everyone knows! Hallelujah!

Brother Dennis called his mother. He told me to call Rhonda Hall, who is Jeremiah Close's mother. Rhonda Hall and her church have been praying incessantly for Alistair. I called her, and we spoke for a long time. We rejoiced together!

She shared so many insightful things with me, and it was wonderful. We shared so many of the same heartaches and a similar joy over Alistair's and Jeremiah's conversions. She will be homeschooling Jeremiah. We will pray about doing it with Alistair.

Hallelujah! Thank You, Lord!

She said that when she first saw Alistair, the Spirit spoke to her and said, "He had a regal look about him, she called him a "Prince of God." God's hand is on him, and He will set men free with His hands, as he is set on fire for the Lord.

She suggested several activities that we might participate in—watching wrestling on campus, prayer walk on campus, preacher boy night, and more.

I called everyone who had stood in the gap with us and told them the good news! Glory to God!

Log Entry: Tuesday, April 30, 2002

And we know that all things work together for good to them that love God, to them who are the called according to his purpose.

Romans 8:28

Jesus will work it out! Glory!

This is the day that the Lord hath made!

I was in Arlington, Virginia, today traveling for my job, and I called Brother Dennis to inquire about Alistair.

I said, "So Brother Dennis, how's Alistair?"

Brother Dennis said, "Oh, Alistair, he's fine! He's doing just fine!" Look at our God!

My heart rejoiced so to see what God is doing in His son, Alistair.

Brother Dennis went on to say that they were tired because they had moved rocks all day for McIntosh Seed Company and had not retuned to campus until 11:30 P.M.

I asked if Alistair had made a public confession yet, and Brother Dennis said no, but Alistair had started smiling without putting his hand over his mouth. "Alistair smiles all the time!"

He has been starting conversations with the other boys.

Alistair told one boy, "I was talking to the devil, and I told him that he couldn't have my soul to send it to hell! Then I went over to Brother Caleb and woke him and told him that I needed to get saved!"

Glory! Hallelujah!

Then (my God! Praises be to God!) Brother Dennis said, "Alistair's countenance has changed. His eyes have changed. Alistair's a good kid, and I am glad to meet Alistair; he's a nice kid."

Oh, my soul rejoices!

Then Brother Dennis said that Alistair is a tireless worker, one of his best workers. Brother Dennis also said that the boys have to minister tonight, and fifteen boys will be sent. The others will remain and move rocks.

Although Alistair would be valuable to Brother Dennis, Brother Dennis asked Alistair if he would like to go and sing. Brother Dennis said he could see that Alistair the "person" was shy, so he asked him just in case Alistair wanted to go but would not volunteer on his own.

When asked, Alistair said, "Yes sir, I would like to go." Brother Dennis said, "All right, then, Alistair."

I recently wrote Alistair a letter telling him to sing unto the Lord and rejoice with his voice.

Visions of Alistair handling the Word and singing before he gives the Word are coming to pass in the natural, as God has already performed them in the supernatural. Thank You, Lord. Amen.

Log Entry: Monday, May 6, 2002

The blood of Jesus still cleanses. It will never lose its power, its miraculous power! It will never lose it!

Log Entry: Friday, May 17, 2002

Recap: On Thursday, May 16, 2002, we caught two planes to Great Falls, Montana, and arrived on time. God is so awesome! (It was exactly eight months since our Alistair left Pennsylvania for the Anchor. Thank You, Lord; eight is the number of new beginnings. This is a new beginning for us.) We asked for a Bonneville and got a Cadillac instead. Look at God! He has done exceeding abundantly above what we could ever ask or think! We went to breakfast and had a lovely ride to Havre with the anticipation of seeing our son. It was the longest thirty-seven miles that I ever traveled.

When we arrived at the Anchor, the boys were finishing recitation. We were told to go into a separate room because they wanted to see how Alistair would react when he saw us. We all thought that it would be all right, but we could not overlook the possible danger that might be expressed against us. Either way, there were young men in close proximity to subdue Alistair if he attacked us.

We waited with great anticipation to see our son. The boys were walking in single file, and Alistair was beckoned to come into the room. He complied.

Alistair came in and looked at me and said, "Hi, Mom." Then he turned and saw his dad, walked over to him, and said, "Hi, Dad," and then put his arms around his dad and hugged him. Alistair's dad hugged him back really hard, and it was a marvelous moment for all of us! Thank You, God!

Brother Dennis told Alistair to go and pack a bag, that he was going to have a visit with his parents.

Alistair looked like he did when we surprised him and his brother by taking them to Disney World. When he was little, he smiled and said, "Are you funning me?" His poor brother started to hyperventilate and exclaim that he could not breathe and that we put his mortal life in danger by surprising him; go figure.

Alistair left the room and was back within a few minutes with a packed bag. We had to encourage him to go back and pack more things, because we were not in a hurry, and we would wait for him. He did.

We drove down the winding highway, and Alistair looked like that little boy on his way to Disney World.

Log Entry: Sunday, May 19, 2002

Sunday morning we were in Hotel 8.

Prayer: There are many things to rejoice about. There is much to pray about.

God: "I will straighten out everything. Sorrow brings about repentance. He cannot return to those same conditions. Things have to change. He is special; I will use him; I will strengthen him in the Word of God. Pray for the following:

- Clarity and comprehension.
- An obedient spirit.
- A compassionate and caring heart.
- Discernment.
- The ability to expound upon and explain the Word of God to anyone.
- Deliverance from deception, lying, false witness, and wanting to see filthy TV programs.
- A spirit of joy.
- A spirit of appreciation."

Me: "Lord, please continue to mold and shape Alistair. We pray in Jesus' name. Amen."

God: "I will deliver and set him free, for I AM God; there is nothing too hard for ME! For this remaining time, I will show you (all) where to go. I will show you (all) what to do. When you return to Philadelphia, Pennsylvania, remember what I said in private."

Me: "Thank YOU, Lord!"

Log Entry: Saturday, May 25, 2005

Recap of last week with Alistair: On Monday, Mountains/Alistair's dad had great conversations with Alistair. On Tuesday, we went to Great Falls, and we saw the Star Wars episode. We saw horses. We had sweet good-byes! Remember, the Lord said that He was going to give us double for our trouble! Glory to God!

Log Entry: Thursday, May 30, 2002

God: "Daughter, you are still a work in progress."

On Thursday evening, we spoke with our Alistair. We had been calling all through the week, but we had been thwarted by interferences. When Alistair came to the telephone, he was the most pleasant that we have ever heard. We laughed and talked!

God is so awesome! God did and is doing a wonderful work in our Alistair.

Alistair was joking and telling us how he was playing basketball and was hit on the head by James. His nose started to bleed profusely. That concerned us, and we just wanted to make sure his nose was not broken.

Alistair is up to Exodus 39 in his Bible reading. Look at God! His voice is a comforting voice. He said that his shoes were falling apart and that he could hear my voice in his head telling him how to stand correctly.

He shared about failing several English and math modules.

Our prayer is for clarity of mind and concentration so that he can absorb the work with ease and comprehend like never before!

This is the new-and-improved Alistair!

It blessed me to hear my baby boy say, "Hi, Mom"!

In addition, when his dad ended the telephone conversation and said, "We love you, Alistair," Alistair said, "I love you too!" He said it unashamedly so!

Thank You, Lord!

YOU are an awesome wonder!

(I read Sister Hughes' letter and the prayer gram again, and it was such a blessing!)

Log Entry: Monday, June 3, 2002

God's promises are true.

We received a very warm, heartfelt letter from our son today. In the letter, Alistair thanked us for coming to visit him. He also said that he had been thinking about us a lot! He referenced how "we/all of us" used to go everywhere together and that after church on Sunday, we used to watch the games . . . ."

Then Alistair said that he wanted to do well in life. He said he was so happy that Son I was doing well in life, and that he wanted to someday succeed well in life also. How humble.

Alistair also asked us to pray for his mind and that he would think good thoughts and be able to concentrate better. Look at God!

His handwriting is better.

Alistair said he is reading his Bible every chance he gets!

When my son closed his letter, he signed it: "With Love, Your Son, Alistair."

His daddy and I rejoiced so! We praise God! Amen!

Log Entry: Friday, June 7, 2002

God: "Alistair is a mighty man of valor!"
Thank You, Lord!

Log Entry: Tuesday, June 11, 2002

The Lord has blessed us so many times! We received a loving and warm letter from our Alistair yesterday, and he has been having some challenges in his schoolwork and has asked us to pray for him. Glory to God! We will! In addition, when I called yesterday, Amy told me that Alistair is now a guide! It has been our heart's desire for Alistair to give something back to the Anchor Academy!

What a privilege! What an honor! Holy, holy is our Lord!

In addition, Alistair said that he stood up on a Wednesday and spoke about that struggle. God is an awesome wonder!

Answered prayer: public testimony (God's way!).

God said: "Write down this prayer because I want you to remember it when I manifest it:

'Strengthen the mind of my Alistair, Lord. Give him a strong and stable mind. Bring Your Word back to his remembrance always. Sharpen his faculties, that he may comprehend all work with godly comprehension. He is (we declare) brilliant! Alistair will teach, orate, explain, and dissect the Word of God! As he is strengthened, he will strengthen others.'"

God said: "I will make Alistair excel in his schoolwork and his understanding. Alistair is a great scholar! Amen."

Log Entry: Later Tuesday, June 11, 2002

Glory!

I spoke with Ms. Sharon today, and she said that Alistair had some educational challenges in biology and math, but he was doing better now. She said that Alistair was always tenacious about his studies even when he initially arrived at the Anchor as a backslider.

She said that he is diligent, and after he failed his PACE test, he came back and requested to take it again. It took all day, but he was faithful and finished! Glory to God!

Alistair was in good spirits, and we spoke about the pictures that he received, his new shoes, and his CD player that we sent to him so that he could listen to Christian CDs. Sending the CD player was not a good idea.

As an aside, Alistair told his dad that it was not good to play video games. (Look at the Lord!) Alistair is a holy young man! Our God answers our prayers! Hallelujah!

Log Entry: Tuesday, June 18, 2002

Holy, holy, holy is the Lord God Almighty!
Thank You, Lord, for this time of visitation!
God: "I am strengthening Alistair right now as we speak."
You must guard your heart and keep your home holy.

We made a horrible mistake, and it cost our Alistair and attributed to his losing ground.

When we sent the same CD player that Alistair used to glorify the devil to the Anchor Academy, the devil used it against him. Although he did not have the actual rap CDs that he used to play on the CD player, that spirit attached to the CD player attacked Alistair, and Alistair started repeating the lyrics again.

God, please forgive my husband and me for lack of discernment!

Victory! Alistair took the CD player and the earphones to Brother Dennis and requested that he keep them for him. Brother Dennis alerted us to what had taken place, and we asked Brother Dennis to destroy it in front of Alistair.

Alistair realized the spiritual implications and turned away from sin! Glory, glory, glory to God!

For a short season, Alistair is alone again. He is not a guide anymore due to his indiscretion. New boys will be coming in, and although we fall down, we get up! Look at our mighty God!

Bless You, Lord, and thank You, Lord! Amen!

Log Entry: Saturday, June 22, 2002

Oh, how we love Jesus because He first loved us! Glory to God! Amen!

Yesterday we received *the* most powerful letter from my Alistair.

Alistair reiterated for his daddy to have a happy Father's Day. (Alistair is happy to have a dad now.) In addition, he said that the letters from Son I were encouraging. He also told us that he had done a dumb thing. (He did not give specifics, but, glory to God, he said that it was a dumb thing!) Amen!

Alistair went on to say that he was no longer a guide, and his level of communication had been dropped. However, he said the next night, for the first time, he gave his testimony! Glory to God!

Then, glory to God, Alistair said, "I am really sorry." Alistair had never said he was sorry about anything.

The sacrifices of God are a broken spirit: a broken
and a contrite heart, O God, thou wilt not despise.
                                        Psalm 51:17

Prayer answered: I asked God for a public testimony from Alistair, and God answered my prayer! Thank You, dear Lord!

Then (hallelujah!), Alistair said, "But I won't give up!"

"I won't give up!" said the young man of God!

Then he said he knew what he did was wrong, and he was sorry that he let God, the staff, Son I, his mom, his dad, and his student down. In addition, he signed his letter, "Love, your son, Alistair."

Thank You, Lord, for the victory we have in Christ. Thank You, Lord, for consecrating this young man for

Yourself. Thank You, Lord, for strengthening Alistair so that he can strengthen another student.

> But as for you, ye thought evil against me; but God meant it unto good, to bring to pass, as it is this day, to save much people alive.
>
> Genesis 50:20

Prayer: That our home would be a holy house, a home where we discard the accursed thing. Glory to God! Help us to subdue our flesh from the pleasures we take in the world!

I contacted the Pennsylvania Christian Home School Organization.

Log Entry: Monday Evening, June 24, 2002

We spoke with Alistair, and he was so elated to tell us that he had gotten back everything that he had lost (i.e., being a guide and a level of communication).

As we talked, he was social. He asked if his dad had gotten rid of the video game system. Alistair considers it an accursed thing.

I believe God is teaching all of us to be holy, not to flirt with sin in any form or fashion. We must be holy; 99.9 percent will not do! "Speak unto all the congregation of the children of Israel, and say unto them, Ye shall be holy: for I the LORD your God am holy" (Leviticus 19:2).

Alistair's new student is Tim, from California. We will pray for Tim.

Alistair went on to say that the staff watches *Gladiator*.

I said, "Oh, that's not a good movie." *(Alistair used to watch it and rewind the stabbing scenes in the movie.)*

He said, "Oh, did you say that for me? It does not affect me that way anymore. I'm not the same person." Then he laughed.

We all laughed.

Then Alistair's dad said, "Oh, you're a 2 Corinthians 5:17 Christian, huh?"

Alistair laughed.

His daddy started repeating 2 Corinthians 5:17 ("Therefore if any man be in Christ, he is a new creature: old things are passed away; behold, all things are become new").

Alistair finished it.

Glory to God! We must continue to thank our mighty God and pray.

Log Entry: Thursday, June 27, 2002

In Luke 12:22-40, what does it mean for us to be ready for Christ's return? Jesus said that instead of worrying about material things, we are to trust God's provision and make HIS kingdom our priority.

Instead of fear that grasps, we are to demonstrate faith that gives.

I prayed for Alistair and for Son I, that they shall by their God run through troops and by their God leap over walls! Glory to God! "For by thee I have run through a troop: by my God have I leaped over a wall" (2 Samuel 22:30).

Log Entry: Saturday, July 6, 2002

The Holy Spirit told me that my Alistair is doing very well.

I am to pray for him because God is going to use his hands to heal soon. A healing hands ministry. Amen.

Log Entry: Sunday, July 7, 2002

Our God is mighty in battle.

Blessed be the name of the Lord!

Prayer: Father, we ask You to restore a great relationship with:

1. Alistair and his pop. Let it be a father and son love story.
2. Alistair and his brother. We ask that their love be the Jesus kind of love between men, that they be devoted to each other like David and Jonathan.
3. Alistair and me, his mom. We ask that Alistair will seek wisdom from me like Solomon sought instruction from his mother. Furthermore, we ask that I will love him enough to know when I must let him go to do Your work.

In Jesus' name, I pray. Amen.

God said: "Look forward to those days with him. They will be wonderful! Enjoy them!"

Log Entry: Monday Evening, July 8, 2002

Glory to God!

We spoke with Son II, the young man of God, and at first, he was a little quiet.

It seemed that his student was having a bad day. How wonderful that Alistair was "feeling" his student's discomfort! Hallelujah!

Alistair said that he had a bad attitude (look at God!). And Alistair had been reading Scriptures to his student about being humble and submissive! Hallelujah!

Our God, the Lord God Almighty, who was, who is, and who always shall be, I AM is a good God!

Thank You, Lord, for confirming Your Word!

God: "Pray for Alistair as I begin to reveal to him his spiritual gifts."

God showed us last evening that He has sharpened Alistair's mind!

Alistair remembered what my most recent letter said.

God has given Alistair a sharp mind concerning the Word of God and his studies. Thank You, Lord!

Log Entry: Wednesday, July 10, 2002

Glory be to God!

We received a letter from our Alistair.

Evidently, the school was driving around looking for somewhere to swim. They found a place with a cliff twenty-five feet above the water.

Alistair said, "Everyone had to drop off the cliff into the water, and needless to say, I was the last one!"

Alistair is so funny! Thank You, Lord!

The Lord God is strengthening Alistair's mind and character, and molding him into the image of Christ!

We pray for the same transformation in my husband, Son I, and me, that we might be on one accord as a family and in ministry.

Tim, James, Michael, and Joshua are new boys at the Anchor; we must pray for them.

Log Entry: Thursday, July 18, 2002

We are more than conquerors through Christ Jesus! Glory to God!

My son recently wrote a letter that touched our hearts so. Alistair said that they needed prayer because the students were misbehaving in the dorms, and everyone suffers when the group, as a whole, does badly. Therefore, Alistair said, "Please pray for us." What a blessing that my boy asked for prayer! Hallelujah! Alistair was learning teamwork; Alistair was caring about someone! Thank You, Lord!

We have been praying (Ephesians 1:15-20; James 1:2-27; 2 Peter 1:2-10).

My Alistair also said that he wanted us to pray for him every day. Ironically, before receiving his letter, I had written to him and told him I pray for him all day and even in my sleep. I am sure that comforted him.

Alistair said, "It must be God! Because I don't deserve any of these positions!" Look at the young man of God! Then he went on to say that he was appreciative that God would even give him one of these jobs, the inference being that, "One is great, but God gave me two!"

My heart is full of gratitude and joy for our Lord! God has diligently answered our prayers to His glory! Thank You, Lord!

Log Entry: Tuesday, July 30, 2002

Holy is the Lord! Amen! Glory to God!

Thank You, Lord! I called Anchor Academy yesterday and found out that Alistair accompanied Brother Trevor and Brother Caleb on tour on the East Coast near our home! Hallelujah!

Alistair requested shirts, and we bought them yesterday. I was told that we could give them to him as we visit the different sites they will be in concert. Also, we were told that we could come as much as we wanted to. Look at God!

We are so grateful to the Lord!

Alistair is getting an education beyond educations, and we are so appreciative!

Now, we need God's total and divine guidance on how we should transition our son back into the fold. Have mercy, Lord, and please guide us with Your own eyes.

Thank You, Lord, and it is in the precious name of our Lord and Savior, Jesus Christ, that we pray and say, "Amen"!

Log Entry: December 2002

Life is wonderful! Alistair came home for Christmas, and we celebrated his birthday (which is not until March 2003). His pre-birthday celebration was a blast! Everyone came to see the young man of God! We called it a 2 Corinthians 5:17 party. He told us that it was the best time of his life!

Log Entry: June 2003

Our Alistair worked feverishly to complete all his schoolwork so he could graduate by June 2003. God is so awesome! Alistair had been left behind in fifth grade, and he would have been nineteen graduating from high school, which is fine, but God made up for the years that the cancer worm destroyed. He found out that if he worked hard, he would be able to graduate on time.

He worked hard, day and night, and he did it! Glory to God!

We traveled to the Anchor for the graduation; we were so proud of him. However, we sensed that Alistair had become smart-mouthed with us. He resembled the insolent boy that we thought was buried and dead. I realized later that I was in denial, but at the time, I wanted the time we spent together to be perfect. God had accomplished the impossible. He saved Alistair's life; He saved his soul, gave him an education beyond belief, and gave him another chance in life. Prior to graduation, Alistair expressed a desire to stay after graduation for several months to help the staff as they transitioned. I was so thankful to God for touching his heart to serve God by serving the Anchor.

Chapter 9

Praising God Always

Log Entry: Saturday, July 5, 2003

God does all things well. On Monday, June 30, 2003, we received a call from Brother Dennis, and we knew by the time, 11:30 P.M. our time, that it was not a good call. Brother Dennis said that there was an integrity issue at hand because Alistair knew that a rap CD had been floating around in the dorm but did not alert the staff about it. (Alistair had volunteered to stay back and help the staff by being a junior staff member at least during the summer months to help as boys were transitioning in and out.) Alistair denied listening to the tape, but admitted to knowing of its existence.

Brother Dennis said that Alistair was *not disrespectful,* but his attitude was a little sullen. (This did not surprise us because when we attended graduation at the school, we saw an Alistair that was similar to the person who attacked his dad but not as hostile. We knew something had happened, but we did not want to think the worst.) I was devastated. Nevertheless, I was moved to back off and let my husband handle everything.

Through many conversations, it was determined that Alistair's heart was not right with God. He had not been reading his Bible and praying. He said he had not listened to the CDs, but we would find out later that he had re-entered that dark world of gangsta rap.

However, when I asked Alistair if he was listening to the CD, he told me, "No," and that he was no longer a Satan worshiper. Glory to God!

Brother Dennis indicated that Alistair might be asked to leave. My heart's desire was for Alistair to stay, serve, and give something back to the Lord. We praise God for the Anchor; God is so good.

Alistair continued to work, and Brother Dennis continued to investigate. Brother Dennis ultimately said that he regained trust in Alistair and offered Alistair the opportunity to repent. Alistair said that he loved God, but he was not ready to repent. Here is an oxymoron. He said that he would like to leave even though they counted him trustworthy again.

God has been so merciful to us.

Our son will start his journey on a train on Monday, July 7, 2003, and will arrive home on Wednesday, July 9, 2003. God said, "It is time. There is still work to do. Stand back, and see the salvation of the Lord. It is well, daughter. It is so well." Amen.

Log Entry: Wednesday, July 9, 2003

God said: "Continue in My direction."
My Alistair is home.

Log Entry: Saturday, July 12, 2003

My husband, sons, Jamal, and Darren went to Promise Keepers in Pittsburgh, Pennsylvania, this weekend. The Lord had me pray Psalm 43. I specifically prayed verse 4: "Then will I go unto the altar of God, unto God my exceeding joy: yea, upon the harp will I praise thee, O God my God."

I prayed that Alistair would take on Jesus in His fullness, that Alistair will accept God's perfect plan for his life, and that Alistair will supernaturally exhibit the joy of the Lord God's love toward him. Amen.

Log Entry: Saturday, August 2, 2003

I belong to God!

All my men are at home today! Oh, how I have prayed for that for two years, that one day God would reunite us as a family.

The oldest son just finished his last message for the youth last night before he returns to IUP for his last semester.

Alistair is a tremendous blessing to our business. He has come home unexpectedly (God knew he would come home when he did) and is getting our rental property up and running.

The Lord said, "This young man is a powerhouse" for Jesus! And we were to continue to preach, teach, and confirm the Word of God in his life. (I believe the Lord wanted to comfort me because I have been seeing some very disturbing things—for example, a spirit of indifference; he looks similar to the old demonic behavior at the genesis of his rebellion. Nevertheless, I believe God!)

In addition, we told him that the courts had released him and that he was no longer on probation, and he was elated. However, it was not necessarily an elation of "thanksgiving" as much as an elation of "I'm free to do what I want to do again!" It seemed like the cover had been taken off and things were about to change. Again, there was no need for restraint.

But as it is written, Eye hath not seen, nor ear heard, neither have entered into the heart of man, the things which God hath prepared for them that love him.

1 Corinthians 2:9

The Lord is going to blow us out of the water with how He will use His Alistair in His ministry. God says he is a "powerhouse"! Alistair is a powerhouse for Jesus! Alistair will be used by our God to be an expression of His compassion, grace, mercy, healing, and deliverance, in Jesus' name! Hallelujah to the Lamb!

Log Entry: Sunday, September 14, 2003

I can of mine own self do nothing: as I hear, I judge: and my judgment is just; because I seek not mine own will, but the will of the Father which hath sent me.

John 5:30

A word from the Lord for my Alistair:

1. I have been long-suffering with you.
2. I have shown you My love, grace, and mercy.
3. I have allowed My servants, your parents, to extend grace, mercy, long-suffering, and unconditional love toward you.
4. You have been deceitful, and the truth is not in you.
5. My mercy will end, just like a thief comes in the night.
6. That is how My Spirit will leave you.
7. I will leave you to your own ways.
8. I have loved you; I have preserved you.
9. Choose this day, choose this day whom you will serve.
10. My judgment will come quickly.
    I AM has spoken.
    Amen.

Log Entry: Monday, September 22, 2003

I just want to say thank You, God, for all You have done for us!

Recap: My son has left the house, returned, and now he is gone again.

God told me the first time when he left that he would return by that Friday, and he did.

However, Alistair got worse and worse . . . .

His behavior was very disrespectful and nasty. Dad stayed up late one night until 2 A.M. ministering to Alistair, and after all the pouring out of his heart, Alistair looked at his dad and said, "You just wasted your time. I am going to listen to rap music, and I will do what I want to do when I am out of your house, but I will follow your rules when I am in your house."

We had to pack him up. We did not feel safe. We were taking turns staying up at night watching our bedroom door because this time, we would not be caught off guard. This time, we would be ready.

Alistair had a clean house, but he opened himself back up to the devil. We begged him not to be like a dog returning to his own vomit. We pleaded with him not to turn back. This time, the enemy came back with seven more vile devils than himself.

Alistair's dad did not want him to be on the streets and insisted that once again he place his baby boy in a soft place to land. Alistair has been at family's home and other places. He may be watching demonic TV programs and other stuff that he wants to, but he is actually in more bondage now than ever before.

God gave me grace to work on the book today even though, once again, my heart is broken. I praised Him for the opportunity to do what He has given me to do.

And I practiced my music. It was accomplishing instead of laborious. My heart is breaking, Lord. I pray, please give me a "want to!"

Log Entry: Wednesday, September 24, 2003

Look what the Lord has done!

I am away traveling for my job, and I have been consecrating myself. The Lord told me, "Daughter, I will give you words to pray, and I only want you to pray the words I say until I change the prayer. Amen."

Under the unction of the Holy Spirit, the following was prayed from the heart: "Once and for all, Lord, I ask Your forgiveness for anything I did not do correctly as a mother. I accept Your forgiveness through the precious blood of my Lord and Savior, Jesus the Christ, who redeemed me from death and purchased everlasting life for me. I release any hurt or disappointment I have taken on by the events (all events) with my son Alistair. I give all of them to You, Lord Jesus. I likewise release my son Alistair **wholly into Your hands!** I will not interfere with Your plan for Alistair anymore. Forgive me, Lord, for walking in the flesh. Have Your perfect way in my son's life. I forgive Alistair.

"Help us (my husband and older son) to be to our Alistair **only** what You would have us to be. Help me to meditate on Your Word, not the natural situation that I see. Show me how to love in spite of how I feel. Thank You, Lord, for Your Romans 8:28 conclusion. Amen."

The Lord had me to bind the spirit of Absalom that was influencing Alistair and to loose the love for God upon him. God encouraged me with His Word: "Alistair will love the Lord God with all his heart, soul, and mind, and he will love his neighbor as himself."

Thank You, great and mighty God!

God said: "Don't doubt! Always look up, daughter!" Amen.

Log Entry: Saturday, October 4, 2003

What a mighty God we serve! Angels bow before Him; heaven and earth adore Him, what a mighty God we serve! Praying in the Spirit...

God: "I AM concerned about everything that concerns you. You feel as though the heavens have closed up unto you, but that is not true. I AM working things to MY perfect will. Rest, and trust ME."

The Lord's Word comforts me.

Psalm 93 (emphasis added):

¹The LORD reigneth [God is in control of the world, and very much so in my life], he is clothed with majesty (He is the King; no one reigns over my God!); the LORD is clothed with strength [He is <u>covered</u> with strength. He is my strength, and if strength covers Him, it covers me too.), wherewith he hath girded himself [He fortified Himself with strength]: the world also is stablished, that it <u>cannot</u> be moved [God's world cannot be shaken. No matter <u>what</u> we see, we are not to be moved from our position of victory in Christ Jesus!).

²Thy throne is established of old [God is the same yesterday, today, and forever. My God does not change His holy attributes]: thou art from everlasting.

³The floods have lifted up [raised up; oh, yes, they seem to be very high for me], O LORD, the floods have lifted up their voice; the floods lift up their waves. [Although it seems like a strong crescendo, it will eventually fall. Waves cannot stand erect for eternity no matter how devastating they may seem

for a season. But God's Word is a garrison around my heart and mind, and I WILL NOT BE MOVED BY MY CIRCUMSTANCES!]

⁴The LORD on high is mightier than the noise of many waters [it sounds terrible, but God wants to know if you'll allow Him to filter out the static], yea, than the mighty waves of the sea [The sea is vast, isn't it? But my God is even <u>more</u> vast than the sea.].
⁵Thy testimonies [Psalm 19:7: "The law of the LORD is perfect, converting the soul: the testimony of the LORD is sure, making wise the simple."] are very sure [certain]: holiness becometh [will appear in] thine house [We receive it, Lord! We could not allow unholiness to reign in and operate with force in our home! God is confirming what He charged us to do!], O LORD, for ever.

GOD: "I WILL MAKE IT RIGHT."

Log Entry: Monday, January 5, 2004

My God is the Creator of all that I purview, the Master Artist, the perfect and Most High God! Glory to God!

Alistair's dad, Son I, David Callaway, and I are on the Triumph Ship, Carnival Line, on our way to San Juan, Puerto Rico. We will also go to St. Thomas and St. Martin.

This trip was originally arranged for Son I's and Son II's graduation (i.e., it was conceived of last April, when we received our tax return. At that time, we vowed that we would go on a cruise with our boys after Son I graduated).

However, things changed. Son II was released from the Anchor for not letting staff know about rap CDs being back on the premises. His dad said that it was time for him to leave. The Anchor did a wonderful, excellent job. God gave

Alistair His best by establishing and allowing the Anchor to exist for saving the lives of young men.

Alistair has since come home, declared that he is unequivocally going to pursue the world's value system, and hence moved in with family.

He is living worldly.

At the height of the drama of this last Exodus, the Lord told me that I would go on the cruise "with joy!"

Recap: As the time neared for the cruise, I was looking for an awesome, external move of God to change Alistair's heart and to give him a renewed mind to make possible his going on the trip with us.

However, in November 2003, the Holy Spirit told me that Peter was to go. He also told my husband that Peter was to go. We therefore extended the offer to Lora, and they eventually accepted.

Also, on Christmas 2003, the Holy Spirit told me that He had a wonderful gift for me concerning Alistair. Oh, how I looked forward to an awesome outpouring of love and reconciliation from my beloved son. Oh, but look at the sovereignty and compassion of my Dad!

The gift was that my heart did not break! When my son of my womb treated me like I was less than an unwanted dog or rat, my heart did not break. Glory to God! The rejection and betrayal did not destroy me. I praise the Lord for such a wonderful gift. Likewise, the pain, hate, rejection, and betrayal did not sap away my husband's joy, either. What a mighty God we serve! God gave us an awesome gift concerning our Alistair . . . He protected our hearts with His love. Thank You, all wise, sovereign, holy, and faithful Lord!

Log Entry: Saturday, February 7, 2004

I just want to say, "Thank You, Lord, for all You have done for me!"

I surrender all to Jesus! That means everything! I surrender my Alistair, Son I, their daddy, and myself. Amen.

The Lord said: "I have an awesome work for the four of you to do. Stay before ME, and get ready! Remember your dog named Beauty? That is just how Alistair's allegiance will be. Amen."

Log Entry: Saturday, February 14, 2004

The Lord said: "Do not fret about Alistair and not being with him in life. When he returns, he will need lots of help. You and his dad will need time to pour into him. So, enjoy this time of freedom and prosperity and ministry."

Log Entry: Monday, April 19, 2004

[1]Wherefore seeing we also are compassed about with so great a cloud of witnesses, let us lay aside every weight, and the sin which doth so easily beset us, and let us run with patience the race that is set before us, [2]looking unto Jesus the author and finisher of our faith; who for the joy that was set before him endured the cross, despising the shame, and is set down at the right hand of the throne of God.

Hebrews 12:1-2

When we visited family, we noticed the CDs that our Alistair has been listening to. Family does not understand that listening to vulgar lyrics is damaging to Alistair and them because those spirits are living in their home.

Alistair does not have to even "hide" anymore.

My husband and I agreed that this situation is just "right" for God! Glory to God!

There is nothing too hard for God!

131

My Alistair will have to meet the Father in a "personal" way.

Log Entry: Tuesday, May 4, 2004

There is not one like the lowly Jesus, no, not one; no, not one.

Alistair spoke to me on the telephone on Sunday afternoon. No telephone hang-ups in my ear. Thank You, Lord! On Sunday morning, Alistair's dad prayed for everyone, and Lena stood proxy for Alistair. Thank You, Lord!

Log Entry: Monday, June 21, 2004

God: "Look at Alistair's pictures. Prophesy to the pictures."

Psalm 47:

[1]O clap your hands, all ye people; shout unto God with the voice of triumph.

[2]For the LORD most high is terrible; he is a great King over all the earth.

[3]He shall subdue the people under us, and the nations under our feet.

[4]He shall choose our inheritance for us, the excellency of Jacob whom he loved. Selah.

[5]God is gone up with a shout, the LORD with the sound of a trumpet.

[6]Sing praises to God, sing praises: sing praises unto our King, sing praises.

[7]For God is the King of all the earth: sing ye praises with understanding.

[8]God reigneth over the heathen: God sitteth upon the throne of his holiness.

⁹The princes of the people are gathered together, even the people of the God of Abraham: for the shields of the earth belong unto God: he is greatly exalted.

Alistair's current state does not move God.
God knows Alistair's end from His beginning.

Log Entry: Monday, July 5, 2004

My God is an awesome wonder!
A woman ran into the back of my car, which left me in pain. My husband and older son saw after me, but Alistair did not even pick up the telephone to inquire if I would live or die. I am grateful for the heart of compassion that GOD is in the process of creating in Alistair. In Jesus' name, I pray, believing those things that are not as if they were! Hallelujah!

I looked through Alistair's pictures again, and they were so beautiful. The Lord cautioned me of the danger and stagnation that comes from living in the past and cautioned me about picturing "the way we were" and said I need to pray about "the way God desires us to be." Glory to God!

Log Entry: Thursday, September 16, 2004

Through every lion-filled den, the Lord has kept me!
Alistair said, "Hello" to me today. Thank You, Lord.

He allowed me to kiss and hug him, and he spoke to me about his pursuit to get an apartment. We offered to help him, and he refused.

We also requested he participate in our twenty-fifth wedding anniversary rededication service, and he said he could not commit. We asked him to take a vacation day. No response.

We would have loved for him to be part of it; we will carry him in our hearts on that day.

Log Entry: Saturday, December 25, 2004

Our God gave us everything in Christ Jesus! We are truly blessed!

We will not be moved by the natural circumstances that surround us! Alistair is saved, in Jesus' name. Our position: We believe God!

Log Entry: Tuesday, May 24, 2005

Lord, I pray that Alistair comes to know You in fullness and joy. I pray that he will preach with power, authority, conviction, and love. Is this my little "Franklin Graham"? Glory to God!

Chapter 10

A Mighty Thing!

Log Entry: Monday, June 6, 2005

Glory to God in the highest! Yesterday the Lord blew us away!

My mother called and told me that Alistair called her to ask for his brother's telephone number. That blessed us so much! Since my mother gave us his cell number, we have called. He never answered his telephone. We left messages of encouragement for him, but none of us ever heard from him. This was wonderful in our sight, and we went about our day!

An hour later, the telephone rang. I heard a conversation that went something like this: "Hello, sir; you want to know who this is? You called me; tell me whom you would like to speak with . . . Hey, Alistair!"

I almost fainted!

Then for approximately five minutes, my husband enjoyed a wonderful, friendly conversation with our Alistair. Alistair's telephone battery went low, and he had to get off the phone, but he said he would call back. Just a little later, Alistair called, and my husband told me to answer the telephone, and I did.

I spoke with a friendly, gracious, confident, and pleasant young man. The last time I saw this person was when he was approximately eight years old. While his dad was speaking with him, I asked the Lord a question: "What are You doing, Lord?"

God answered, "Being God."

I said, "Hallelujah!"

We talked about where he lived, where he was going to move to, where he was going to school, how he was, his health, dental concerns, how he was eating, and so on.

We were so blessed, and I grinned during the entire conversation.

Alistair said that he and his brother made a date to hang out together on Friday, June 17, 2005. His dad invited him to Father's Day dinner, and he said he would like to attend.

We mentioned the Anchor Academy staff to him, and he said, "Wow, you all still stay in touch with them?" We replied, "Yes." He replied, "That's nice."

Alistair got off the telephone because he was to catch a bus. However, when he arrived home, he called us again and requested the telephone number for the Anchor Academy. Glory to God! Alistair had hated the Anchor Academy for Boys, his parents, his brother, and God. The Lord reconnected him with Himself, his brother, his parents, and the Anchor. Look at God!

We had to allow the sin to run its course. It was painful, but necessary.

When the Lord Jesus hung on a tree for our sins, it was painful for Him, but necessary for our salvation.

Thank You, Lord, for speaking the Anchor Academy for Boys into existence.

Thank You, Lord, for bringing all in my family to the end of self.

Thank You, Lord, for being so merciful and gracious unto all of us sinners.

Thank You, Lord, for preserving our lives to serve You.

Thank You, Lord, for bringing us back together as a family to worship and serve You and to serve Your people.

Thank You for being faithful to us, Lord! You said You would save our son and brother, and You did!

We thank You, Lord, and praise You for this great and mighty thing You have done! It is truly marvelous in our sight! We love You, Lord! And it is in the mighty name of Jesus the Christ we thank You and pray. Amen.

Epilogue

Glory to God!

Alistair had Father's Day dinner with us, and I do not ever remember seeing my husband happier. In the weeks to come, he called his dad and inquired about the time of new member classes and church services at our church, where my husband is the pastor. He has attended Sunday morning service, Wednesday prayer and Bible study, and men's fellowship services ever since. He's being trained to be part of the church security team and serves as a greeter. After every Sunday service, he comes home and has supper with us.

Alistair is a Bible-believing, Bible-quoting, and will-not-be-beguiled Christian. We are still praying for him in the area of compassion because as he ministers Christ to young men with his dad, he can only take but so much before he tells them, "Get right with Jesus, or you are going straight to hell!"

Alistair knows the truth and the Word of God taught to him at an early age and specifically at the Anchor, which was his anchor. Everything God deposited in Alistair at the Anchor and in his youth is bringing forth fruit!

Today, Alistair serves his country as a member of the United States Marine Corps, whose motto is "Semper fidelis," Latin for "always faithful." Thank You, Lord, and thank you, Anchor Academy for Boys, for being always faithful!

Fight to Win

Forgiveness is so costly due to the crime, it's as if the pain
    will never leave your mind.
Thoughts of rage surface still, feeling as though you could kill.
Will these things leave my mind?
Is this what children do in their spare time?
Thinking they raised themselves and all
Just because you've grown up so tall.
What does the Bible say in response to it all?

Honor, obey are two things that stand in your way
Of destroying your life and living just for the day.
Your parents, the vessels used to usher you in,
To teach you how to live for God so you could win.
What will it take for you to see
The enemy of your mind is the devil, not me?

So fight; you can win, with Jesus on your side.
It's your soul; don't let Satan take you for a ride.
Get a grip; don't trip; the test has just begun.
Put on your helmet, the shield of faith; the battle can be won.
Check your shoes; unsheathe your sword; now you've got
    him on the run.
Speak the Word with boldness; you're right on edge.
Victory is near, and the enemy is feeling dread.
Swing with all your might; don't lose this fight.
Stay on your knees in prayer tonight.

No weapon that forms against you can win.
Every tongue that rises in judgment, you shall condemn.
God's given angels charge over you to defend,
To keep you from falling and not getting up again.

Where's your faith small as mustard seed?
He said it's just enough so you can succeed.
Take heart; you have little strength; don't give up.
You can do all things through Christ; surely, that's enough!

Jesus—the name with all power.
Nothing else will do in this hour.
His mercy endures.
His grace is sufficient.
So get up and win this mission!

—Anonymous

SCRIPTURES TO BUILD YOUR FAITH AND STRENGTHEN YOU

1. "Bless the LORD, ye his angels, that excel in strength, that do his commandments, hearkening unto the voice of his word" (Psalm 103:20).

2. "So then faith cometh by hearing, and hearing by the word of God" (Romans 10:17).

3. "He that spareth his rod hateth his son: but he that loveth him chasteneth him betimes" (Proverbs 13:24).

4. "For the preaching of the cross is to them that perish foolishness; but unto us which are saved it is the power of God" (1 Corinthians 1:18).

5. "For whatsoever is born of God overcometh the world: and this is the victory that overcometh the world, even our faith" (1 John 5:4).

6. "For it was not an enemy that reproached me; then I could have borne it; neither was it he that hated me that did magnify himself against me; then I would have hid myself from him: But it was thou, a man mine equal, my guide, and mine acquaintance. We took sweet counsel together, and walked unto the house of God in company" (Psalm 55:12-14).

7. "Casting all your care [throw it] upon him [the Lord Jesus]; for he careth for you" (1 Peter 5:7).

8. "Delight thyself also in the LORD: and he shall give thee the desires of thine heart" (Psalm 37:4).

9. "Jesus saith unto him, I am the way, the truth, and the life: no man cometh unto the Father, but by me" (John 14:6).

10. "Children, obey your parents in the Lord: for this is right. Honour thy father and mother; which is the first commandment with promise; that it may be well with thee, and thou mayest live long on the earth" (Ephesians 6:1-3).

11. "If we confess our sins, he is faithful and just to forgive us our sins, and to cleanse us from all unrighteousness" (1 John 1:9).

12. "Howbeit when he, the Spirit of truth, is come, he will guide you into all truth: for he shall not speak of himself; but whatsoever he shall hear, that shall he speak: and he will shew you things to come" (John 16:13).

13. "A wise son heareth his father's instruction: but a scorner heareth not rebuke" (Proverbs 13:1).

14. "Train up a child in the way he should go: and when he is old, he will not depart from it" (Proverbs 22:6).

15. "And all thy children shall be taught of the LORD; and great shall be the peace of thy children" (Isaiah 54:13).

16. "Fathers, provoke not your children to anger, lest they be discouraged" (Colossians 3:21).

17. "Then said the LORD unto me, Thou hast well seen: for I will hasten my word to perform it" (Jeremiah 1:12).

18. "And he shall turn the heart of the fathers to the children, and the heart of the children to their fathers, lest I come and smite the earth with a curse" (Malachi 4:6).

19. "This is the day which the LORD hath made; we will rejoice and be glad in it" (Psalm 118:24).

20. "Strength and honour are her clothing; and she shall rejoice in time to come. She openeth her mouth with wisdom; and in her tongue is the law of kindness. She looketh well to the ways of her household, and eateth not the bread of idleness. Her children arise up, and call her blessed; her husband also, and he praiseth her" (Proverbs 31:25-28).

21. "Wherefore seeing we also are compassed about with so great a cloud of witnesses, let us lay aside every weight, and the sin which doth so easily beset us, and let us run with patience the race that is set before us, looking unto Jesus the author and finisher of our faith; who for the joy that was set before him endured the cross, despising the shame, and is set down at the right hand of the throne of God. For consider him that endured such contradiction of sinners against himself, lest ye be wearied and faint in your minds. Ye have not yet resisted unto blood, striving against sin" (Hebrews 12:1-4).

22. "If ye endure chastening, God dealeth with you as with sons; for what son is he whom the father chasteneth

not? For they verily for a few days chastened us after their own pleasure; but he for our profit, that we might be partakers of his holiness. Now no chastening for the present seemeth to be joyous, but grievous: nevertheless afterward it yieldeth the peaceable fruit of righteousness unto them which are exercised thereby. Wherefore lift up the hands which hang down, and the feeble knees; and make straight paths for your feet, lest that which is lame be turned out of the way; but let it rather be healed" (Hebrews 12:7, 10-13).

23. "And I, if I be lifted up from the earth, will draw all men unto me" (John 12:32).

24. "The king's heart is in the hand of the LORD, as the rivers of water: he turneth it whithersoever he will" (Proverbs 21:1).

25. "For I know the thoughts that I think toward you, saith the LORD, thoughts of peace, and not of evil, to give you an expected end [hope in your latter end]. Then shall ye call upon me, and ye shall go and pray unto me, and I will hearken unto you. And ye shall seek me, and find me, when ye shall search for me with all your heart. And I will be found of you, saith the LORD: and I will turn away your captivity, and I will gather you from all the nations, and from all the places whither I have driven you, saith the LORD; and I will bring you again into the place whence I caused you to be carried away captive" (Jeremiah 29:11-14).

26. "To whom then will ye liken God? or what likeness will ye compare unto him?" (Isaiah 40:18).

27. "Hast thou not known? hast thou not heard, that the ever-lasting God, the LORD, the Creator of the ends of the earth, fainteth not, neither is weary? there is no searching of his understanding" (Isaiah 40:28).

28. "He giveth power to the faint; and to them that have no might he increaseth strength" (Isaiah 40:29).

29. "But they that wait upon the LORD shall renew their strength; they shall mount up with wings as eagles; they shall run, and not be weary; and they shall walk, and not faint" (Isaiah 40:31).

30. "But as it is written, Eye hath not seen, nor ear heard, neither have entered into the heart of man, the things which God hath prepared for them that love him" (1 Corinthians 2:9).

31. "And now, Lord, what wait I for? my hope is in thee" (Psalm 39:7).

32. "Let us therefore come boldly unto the throne of grace, that we may obtain mercy, and find grace to help in time of need" (Hebrews 4:16).

33. "And I sought for a man among them, that should make up the hedge, and stand in the gap before me for the land, that I should not destroy it: but I found none" (Ezekiel 22:30).

34. "A new heart also will I give you, and a new spirit will I put within you: and I will take away the stony heart out of your flesh, and I will give you an heart of flesh. And I will put my spirit within you, and cause you to walk in my statutes, and ye shall keep my judgments, and do

them. And ye shall dwell in the land that I gave to your fathers; and ye shall be my people, and I will be your God" (Ezekiel 36:26-28).

35. "Likewise the Spirit also helpeth our infirmities: for we know not what we should pray for as we ought: but the Spirit itself maketh intercession for us with groanings which cannot be uttered" (Romans 8:26).

36. "Is not this the fast that I have chosen? to loose the bands of wickedness, to undo the heavy burdens, and to let the oppressed go free, and that ye break every yoke?" (Isaiah 58:6).

37. "Therefore if any man be in Christ, he is a new creature: old things are passed away; behold, all things are become new" (2 Corinthians 5:17).

38. "For this cause we also, since the day we heard it, do not cease to pray for you, and to desire that ye might be filled with the knowledge of his will in all wisdom and spiritual understanding; that ye might walk worthy of the Lord unto all pleasing, being fruitful in every good work, and increasing in the knowledge of GOD; strengthened with all might, according to HIS glorious power, unto all patience and longsuffering with joyfulness; giving thanks unto the Father, which hath made us meet [fit] to be partakers of the inheritance of the saints in light: who hath delivered us from the power of darkness, and hath translated us into the kingdom of his dear Son: in whom we have redemption [been set free] through HIS blood, even the forgiveness of sins" (Colossians 1:9-14, emphasis added).

39. "For by grace are ye saved through faith; and that not of yourselves: it is the gift of God: not of works, lest any man should boast" (Ephesians 2:8-9).

40. "That if thou shalt confess with thy mouth the Lord Jesus, and shalt believe in thine heart that God hath raised him from the dead, thou shalt be saved" (Romans 10:9).

41. "For all the promises of God in him are yea, and in him amen, unto the glory of God by us" (2 Corinthians 1:20).

9 781615 799473